First World War
and Army of Occupation
War Diary
France, Belgium and Germany

1 INDIAN CAVALRY DIVISION
Lucknow Cavalry Brigade,
Brigade Supply Officer
and Brigade Transport Officer
30 July 1914 - 28 September 1916

WO95/1175/6

The Naval & Military Press Ltd
www.nmarchive.com
Published in association with The National Archives

Published by

The Naval & Military Press Ltd

Unit 10 Ridgewood Industrial Park,

Uckfield, East Sussex,

TN22 5QE England

Tel: +44 (0) 1825 749494

www.naval-military-press.com

www.nmarchive.com

This diary has been reprinted in facsimile from the original. Any imperfections are inevitably reproduced and the quality may fall short of modern type and cartographic standards.

© Crown Copyright
Images reproduced by permission of The National Archives, London, England, 2015.

Contents

Document type	Place/Title	Date From	Date To
Heading	WO95/1175/6		
Heading	BEF 1 Ind. Cav Div Supply Officer Lucknow Bde 1914 Aug To 1916 Sept		
Heading	War Diary of Supply Officer Lucknow Cavalry Brigade From 30th July 1914 to 31st December 1914		
War Diary		30/07/1914	31/12/1914
Heading	War Diary with Appendices of Brigade Supply Officer; Lucknow Cavalry Brigade From 1st March 1915 To 31st March 1915		
War Diary	Heuchin	01/03/1915	07/03/1915
War Diary	Febvin	08/03/1915	11/03/1915
War Diary	Lapugnoy	11/03/1915	11/03/1915
War Diary	Auchel	12/03/1915	14/03/1915
War Diary	Febvin	17/03/1915	18/03/1915
War Diary	Estree Blanche	18/03/1915	31/03/1915
Miscellaneous	Messages. Signals And Field Telegraphs.		
Miscellaneous	Instructions. Appx 1		
Miscellaneous	Messages, Signals And Field Telegraphs.		
Miscellaneous	Instructions. Appx 2		
Miscellaneous	Messages, Signals And Field Telegraphs.		
Miscellaneous	Instructions. Appx 3		
Miscellaneous	Messages, Signals And Field Telegraphs.		
Miscellaneous	Instructions. Appx 4		
Miscellaneous	Messages, Signals And Field Telegraphs.		
Miscellaneous	Instructions. Appx 5		
Miscellaneous	Messages, Signals And Field Telegraphs.		
Miscellaneous	Instructions. Appx 6		
Miscellaneous	Messages. Signals And Field Telegraphs.		
Miscellaneous	Instructions. Appx VII		
Operation(al) Order(s)	Operation Order No. 1 by Br. Gen. Fasken, Comdg. Lucknow Cavalry Brigade	10/03/1915	10/03/1915
Miscellaneous	A Form. Messages And Signals.		
Miscellaneous	Messages, Signals And Field Telegraphs.		
Miscellaneous	Instructions		
Miscellaneous	Messages, Signals And Field Telegraphs.		
Miscellaneous	Instructions		
Miscellaneous	Messages, Signals And Field Telegraphs.		
Miscellaneous	Instructions		
Miscellaneous	Messages, Signals And Field Telegraphs.		
Miscellaneous	Instructions		
Miscellaneous	Messages, Signals And Field Telegraphs.		
Miscellaneous	Instructions		
Miscellaneous	A Form. Messages And Signals.		
Miscellaneous			
Miscellaneous	A Form. Messages And Signals.		
Heading	War Diary of Supply Officer Lucknow Cavalry Brigade, 1st Indian Cavalry Division From 1st February 1915 To 28th February 1915		
War Diary	Heuchin Pas-De-Calais	03/02/1915	06/02/1915
War Diary		01/02/1915	28/02/1915

War Diary	Heuchin	01/01/1915	31/01/1915
Heading	War Diary of Brigade Supply Officer Lucknow Cavalry Brigade 1st Indian Cavalry Division From 1st January 1915 To 31st January 1915		
Heading	War Diary of Supply Officer Lucknow Cavalry Brigade From 1st April 1915 To 30th April 1915		
War Diary	Estree Blanche	01/04/1915	24/04/1915
War Diary	Oxelaere	25/04/1915	27/04/1915
War Diary	St. Jans Ter Biezen	27/04/1915	30/04/1915
Heading	War Diary of Brigade Supply Officer Lucknow Cavalry Brigade. From 1st May 1915 To 31st May 1915		
War Diary	St Jan Ter Biezen	01/05/1915	31/05/1915
Heading	War Diary of Supply Officer, Lucknow Cavalry Brigade From 1st August 1915 To 31st August 1915		
War Diary		01/08/1915	30/08/1915
Heading	War Diary of Supply Officer, Lucknow Cavalry Brigade From 1st September 1915 To 30th September 1915		
War Diary		01/09/1915	30/09/1915
Heading	War Diary of Supply Officer, Lucknow Cavalry Brigade From 1st October 1915 To 31st December 1915		
War Diary		10/10/1915	31/12/1915
Heading	War Diary of Supply Officer, Lucknow Cavalry Brigade From 1st January 1916 To 31st January 1916		
War Diary		01/01/1916	31/01/1916
Heading	War Diary of Supply Officer, Lucknow Cavalry Brigade From 1st February 1916 To 29th February 1916		
War Diary		01/02/1916	03/03/1916
Heading	War Diary of Supply Officer Lucknow Cavalry Brigade From 1st March 1916 To 31st March 1916		
War Diary		04/03/1916	26/03/1916
War Diary	Vaulx	26/03/1916	29/03/1916
Heading	War Diary of Brigade Supply Officer Lucknow Cavalry Brigade From 1st April 1916 To 30th April 1916		
War Diary	Vaulx	01/04/1916	07/04/1916
War Diary	Yvrench	08/04/1916	14/04/1916
War Diary	Vaulx	10/04/1916	30/04/1916
Heading	War Diary of Supply Officer, Lucknow Cavalry Brigade From 1st May 1916 To 31st May 1916		
War Diary	St Riquier	01/05/1916	06/05/1916
War Diary	Vaulx	07/05/1916	09/05/1916
War Diary	Rebreuve	10/05/1916	31/05/1916
War Diary	War Diary of Supply Officer, Lucknow Cavalry Brigade From 1st June 1916 To 30th June 1916		
War Diary	Rebreuve	01/06/1916	30/06/1916
Heading	War Diary of Supply Officer, Lucknow Cavalry Brigade From 1st July 1916 To 31st July 1916		
War Diary	Grouches	01/07/1916	01/07/1916
War Diary	Frohen-Le-Grand	01/07/1916	18/07/1916
War Diary	Villers-Brulin	19/07/1916	30/07/1916
War Diary	Chellers	31/07/1916	31/07/1916
Heading	War Diary of Supply Officer, Lucknow Cavalry Brigade From 1st August 1916 To 31st August 1916		
War Diary	Chellers	01/08/1916	08/08/1916

War Diary	Pas	09/08/1916	31/08/1916
Heading	War Diary of Supply Officer, Lucknow Cavalry Brigade From 1st September 1916 To 30th September 1916		
War Diary	Pas	01/09/1916	02/09/1916
War Diary	Occoches	02/09/1916	03/09/1916
War Diary	Brailly	04/09/1916	10/09/1916
War Diary	Frohen Le GD	11/09/1916	11/09/1916
War Diary	Hem	12/09/1916	12/09/1916
War Diary	Querrieux	13/09/1916	13/09/1916
War Diary	Albert	15/09/1916	15/09/1916
War Diary	Montauban	26/09/1916	26/09/1916
War Diary	Bussy-Les-Daours.	27/09/1916	27/09/1916
War Diary	Hangest Sur Somme	28/09/1916	28/09/1916
War Diary	Bois de L'abbaye	29/09/1916	29/09/1916
War Diary	Crecy en Ponthied	30/09/1916	30/09/1916
War Diary	WO95/1175/7		
Heading	B.E.F. 1 Ind. Cav. Div. Lucknow Bde. Bde Transport Officer 1914 Nov-1915 July 1916 July-1916 Sept		
Heading	War Diary of Lucknow Bgde Transport Officer From 16-11-14 To 25-12-14		
War Diary	Orleans	16/11/1914	08/12/1914
War Diary	Lillers	14/12/1914	22/12/1914
War Diary	Heuchin	25/12/1914	25/12/1914
War Diary	War Diary of Brigade Transport, Lucknow Cavalry Brigade From 1-1-15 To 31-1-15		
War Diary	Heuchin	01/01/1915	08/01/1915
War Diary	Manlers	09/01/1915	09/01/1915
War Diary	Festubert	09/01/1915	11/01/1915
War Diary	Bethune	12/01/1915	12/01/1915
War Diary	Heuchin	18/01/1915	31/01/1915
Heading	War Diary of Brigade Transport Officer, Lucknow Cavalry Brigade From 1st February 1915 To 28th February 1915		
War Diary	Heuchin	01/02/1915	28/02/1915
Heading	War Diary of Brigade Transport Officer Lucknow Cavalry Brigade From 22nd April 1915 To 30th April 1915		
War Diary	Estree Blanche	22/04/1915	24/04/1915
War Diary	St Marie Cappel	25/04/1915	29/04/1915
War Diary	St Jan-Ter-Biezen	30/04/1915	30/04/1915
War Diary	War Diary of Transport (Lucknow Cavalry Brigade) Head Quarters From 1st May 1915 To 31st May 1915		
War Diary	St Jan-Ter-Biezen	01/05/1915	04/05/1915
War Diary	St Marie Cappel	05/05/1915	05/05/1915
War Diary	Mametz	06/05/1915	28/05/1915
War Diary	L'Erkels Brugge	29/05/1915	31/05/1915
War Diary	War Diary Transport Officer Lucknow Cavalry Brigade From 1st June 1915 To 30th June 1915		
War Diary	L'Erkels Brugge	01/06/1915	14/06/1915
War Diary	Mametz	15/06/1915	30/06/1915
Heading	War Diary of Transport Officer Lucknow Cavalry Brigade From 1st July 1915 To 31st July 1915		
War Diary	Mametz	01/07/1915	31/07/1915
War Diary	War Diary of Transport Officer, Lucknow Cavalry Brigade From 1st July 1916 To 31st July 1916		

War Diary		02/07/1916	25/07/1916
Heading	War Diary of Transport Officer Lucknow Cavalry Brigade From 1st August 1916 To 31st August 1916		
War Diary	France	06/08/1916	31/08/1916
Heading	War Diary of Transport Officer, Lucknow Cavalry Brigade From 1st September 1916 To 30th September 1916		
War Diary	Pas	01/09/1916	30/09/1916
Heading	War Diary of 14th To 28.9.16 (September) 1916		
War Diary	St Gratien	14/09/1916	14/09/1916
War Diary	Querieu	17/09/1916	28/09/1916

WO 95/11756 9/15/6

BEF

1 Ind. Cav Div

Supply Officer

Lucknow Bde

~~1915 Aug~~ to 1916 Sept
1914 Aug

(No ~~Box~~)

WAR DIARY

of

Supply Officer Lucknow Cavalry Brigade

from 30th July 1914 to 31st December 1914.

Army Form C. 2118.

WAR DIARY
or
INTELLIGENCE SUMMARY.

(Erase heading not required.)

Instructions regarding War Diaries and Intelligence
Summaries are contained in F. S. Regs., Part II.
and the Staff Manual respectively. Title pages
will be prepared in manuscript.

[Stamp: ADJUTANT GENERAL IN INDIA / BASE OFFICE / 26 JAN 1915]

Hour, Date, Place.	Summary of Events and Information	Remarks and references to Appendices.
30 July 19 14	Received orders to proceed to Bombay to embark for field service orders of A.D. of troops no IV Bombay	
31st July 15 14	Proceeded to Bombay.	
2nd August to 14 14	Arrive at Bombay	
2nd August — 18th October	Awaited orders to embark	
15th October 14	left Bombay on H.t. transport "Tony Merchant" owing to ship heating down transhipped to the P.&O. S.S. Kittan	
7th November 14	Arrived at Marseilles.	
10 November 14	left Marseilles for Orleans	

Army Form C. 2118.

WAR DIARY
or
INTELLIGENCE SUMMARY.
(Erase heading not required.)

Instructions regarding War Diaries and Intelligence Summaries are contained in F. S. Regs., Part II, and the Staff Manual respectively. Title pages will be prepared in manuscript.

Hour, Date, Place.	Summary of Events and Information	Remarks and references to Appendices.
October, November 1914	Arrived Orleans —	
14th November 14	Received orders to turn Orleans from B.S. of supplies into of Communication depot equipment.	
15th November 14	Arrived Lasalles —	
16 – 23rd Nov: 14	Awaited arrival of system and when it came per arrived forwarded same to Orleans	
23rd November 14	left Lasalles	
24th " 14	arrived Orleans reported by arrival the G.O.C. of the formation, who had been appointed early Reckon Cavalry Brigade as supply and Reposition officer.	

Gulab Singh & Sons, Calcutta—No. 22 Army C.—5-8-14—1,07,000.

Army Form C. 2118.

WAR DIARY
or
INTELLIGENCE SUMMARY.

(Erase heading not required.)

Instructions regarding War Diaries and Intelligence Summaries are contained in F. S. Regs., Part II, and the Staff Manual respectively. Title pages will be prepared in manuscript.

Hour, Date, Place.	Summary of Events and Information	Remarks and references to Appendices.
25th November 1914	Proceeded with advance party of brigade to H.Q Oner and after receiving orders proceeded to Lillers. — LILLERS.	
26 November 1914	Travelling — arrived LILLERS —	
27		
28		
29		
30	Carried on routine duties —	
1		
2		
3		
4		
5		
6		
7		
8		

Army Form C. 2118.

WAR DIARY
or
INTELLIGENCE SUMMARY.

(Erase heading not required.)

Instructions regarding War Diaries and Intelligence Summaries are contained in F. S. Regs., Part II, and the Staff Manual respectively. Title pages will be prepared in manuscript.

Hour, Date, Place.	Summary of Events and Information	Remarks and references to Appendices.
8th December 1914	Brigade arrived at Lillers —	
9/10		
11		
12		
13		
14	carried on routine duties.	
15		
16		
17		
18		
19		
20		
21		
22 " December "	Left billets at LILLERS, proceeded to NORRENT-FONTES.	
23–24 "	routine duties	

Army Form C. 2118.

WAR DIARY
or
INTELLIGENCE SUMMARY.

(Erase heading not required.)

Instructions regarding War Diaries and Intelligence Summaries are contained in F. S. Regs., Part II, and the Staff Manual respectively. Title pages will be prepared in manuscript.

Hour, Date, Place.	Summary of Events and Information	Remarks and references to Appendices.
25th December 1914	Left NOARENT FONTES. arrived at HEUCHIN.	
26		
27		
28	Carried out routine duties	
29		
30		
31		

R.D. No 75
22/1/15.

J. Sell. Kincaid
Captain
Supply Officer
Lucknow Cav: Brigade

WAR DIARY

with Appendices.

of

Brigade Supply Officer, Lucknow Cavalry Brigade.

From 1st March 1915 to 31st March 1915.

Army Form C. 2118.

Brigade Supply Officer
Lucknow Cavalry Brigade

WAR DIARY

~~INTELLIGENCE SUMMARY~~

(Erase heading not required.)

Instructions regarding War Diaries and Intelligence Summaries are contained in F. S. Regs., Part II. and the Staff Manual respectively. Title pages will be prepared in manuscript.

Hour, Date, Place	Summary of Events and Information	Remarks and references to Appendices
HEUCHIN MARCH 1st–15	Routine duties in Billets	

[Stamp: ADJUTANT GENERAL INDIA — 11. APR 1915 — BASE OFFICE]

Army Form C. 2118.

Brigade Supply Officer
Lucknow Cavalry Brigade

WAR DIARY
INTELLIGENCE SUMMARY
(Erase heading not required.)

Instructions regarding War Diaries and Intelligence Summaries are contained in F.S. Regs., Part II. and the Staff Manual respectively. Title pages will be prepared in manuscript.

Hour, Date, Place		Summary of Events and Information	Remarks and references to Appendices
March 7	2.30pm HEUCHIN	Received instructions that units will move into Close Billets in area PALFART - LIVOSSART - FEBVIN and FONTAIN - LEZ-HERMANS. While units were moving proceeded to NORRENT-FONTES to discuss arrangements for feeding Supply tomorrow, on return received instructions to withdraw Supply tomorrow at NORRENT-FONTES. Supply HQ at FEBVIN after dark.	AAQMG 1st I.A. Corr. Q.1349 of 7.3.15 - 7.30pm Appx I
March 8	FEBVIN	Senr Sgt. Bettoswill with in AT Coult. to HEUCHIN to bring in surplus stores left behind. Proceeded there personally and kissa 2 country carts to bring into FEBVIN our hay previously purchased. Paid bills to HEUCHIN and CREPY. Lorries were drawn at 6.15pm.	Appx II AAQMG 1st I.C. Q.1355 of 8.3.15 Appx III AAQMG 1st I.C. Q.1362 d.8.3.15 7.28pm
	8pm	Received instructions that nuclegors (on orders will be ??) at 2pm	Orders re AUCHY AUX BOIS
March 9			Appx IV
	6pm	Supply lorries were unloaded except hay all lorries except hay returned	AAQMG 1st I.C. Q.1373 d.9.3.15 Appx XI HAQMG. 1st I.C. Q.1374 d.9.3.15
	11pm	Hay lorries unloaded and returned.	
March 10	11.am.	Received orders for final arrangements at AUCHY AUX BOIS. Orders received 2pm	Appx VI AAQMG 1st I.C. Q.1376 d.10.2.15
	6.45pm	Lorries unloaded and returned.	AAQMG 1st I.C. Q.1385 d.10.3.15 Appx XVIII
	10.25pm	Orders received for march to MARLES tomorrow morning at 1.30 am	Appx 8. Return Pub. Operator in Cin. No. I. Oalww 10.3.15 Esay no. 6.
March 11	6 am.	Handed over surplus stores to Mayor of FEBVIN and proceeded to MARLES. Brought in horse hay for unit from LA BOEUVRIERE & LABUSNOY. Un... Pass had not the also our Army Pro-Pr N. Balo for Hd.qr in ...	AQQMG 1st I.C. no Q.13 87 of 10.3.15

Army Form C. 2118.

WAR DIARY
or
INTELLIGENCE SUMMARY

(Erase heading not required.)

Brigade Supply Officer
Lahore Cavalry Brigade

Instructions regarding War Diaries and Intelligence Summaries are contained in F. S. Regs., Part II. and the Staff Manual respectively. Title pages will be prepared in manuscript.

Hour, Date, Place	Summary of Events and Information	Remarks and references to Appendices
LAPUGNOY 11 March 3 p.m.	Informed Hd. Qrs waggons would be at S.W. end of MARLES at 5 p.m. at S.W. end of MARLES Horse T.	A.A.Q.M.G. 1352 C. Q. 1388 d. 11.3.15 1.55 p.m.
4.5 p.m.	Left Supply units for Horse waggons at A.T. Cooks with BDE WG	
	B.A.T. Cooker rpt. and 2 pm H.D.Qr's and church'in Hrs Rprossed k	
	Church MARLES and parked lorries her and took on supplies	
	Transactions completed at 9.30 p.m.	
AUCHEL 12.3.15 10.30 a.m.	Informed Final Rendezvous at N. end of RAIMBERT at 3 p.m.	G.A. 162 d. 12.3.15 A G S 01 1 p.m.
12.30 p.m.	B.S.O. proceeded R. Bullet. t. AUCHEL	
	Met lorries at 3 p.m. and Issc. transferrially funds. Supplies & units	
	completed 5 p.m. and all lorries returned again to D.A.Q.M.G.	
AUCHEL 13.3.15		
10.45 a.m.	Information received transfrognons at M. end of RAIMBERT at 3 p.m.	A.A.Q.M.G. 1341 C.D. Q.1406 d 13 3/15
4.45 p.m.	Lorries dismissed.	
AUCHEL 14.3.15		A.A.Q.M.G. 01 9.C.D. Q.1410 d.13 3/15
11.10 a.m.	Informed Final R.V. for S.C. N end of RAIMBERT 3 p.m.	A.A.Q.M.G. 1417 14/15
11.30 a.m.	Above order cancelled.	A.A.Q.M.G. 1418 14 3/15
1 p.m.	Lorries will deliver early tomorrow morning.	" " 1415 " "
	R.V. at NORRENT FONTES. Lorries Dismissed.	" " 1423 " "
5.37 p.m.	Received Bde will move about 10 am. Transp. at 10 p.m.	P.M. 27 14/15
7 p.m.	Received orders to march to FEBVIN. Proceeded there	

1247 W 8299 200,000 (E) 8/14 J.B.C. & A. Forms/C. 2118/11.

Army Form C. 2118.

WAR DIARY
or
INTELLIGENCE SUMMARY

(Erase heading not required.)

Instructions regarding War Diaries and Intelligence Summaries are contained in F. S. Regs., Part II. and the Staff Manual respectively. Title pages will be prepared in manuscript.

Hour, Date, Place	Summary of Events and Information	Remarks and references to Appendices
FEBVIN 17.3.15 6.30 pm.	Orders issued for change of billets tomorrow as follows. H.D.Qrs. LONGHEM. 2/9 Lancers ESTÉE BLANCHE and FLECHINELLE 3/6 Jacob Horse LIETTRES and LINGHEM K.D.Guides FLECHIN and CUHEM.	B.M. 46 & 17 3/15
18.3.15 10.10 am	Bde moved off from Bruin	
Estrée Blanche 18.3.15	} Routine duties in Billets	
to		
31.3.15		

Amrit Teer Captain
Bde Supply Officer
Lucknow Cavalry Brigade

1247 W 3299 200,000 (E) 8/14 J.B.C. & A. Forms/C. 2118/11.

MESSAGES, SIGNALS AND FIELD TELEGRAPHS.

Army Form C. 2121. Modified for India.

No. of Message 56

Prefix SM Code EP m. Words 47 Charge. (X) For Stamps. Recd. 1.40 p m.
Office of Origin and Service Instructions.
VIA — Three adds
Sent. At ___ m. To ___ By ___
Date P1B 7/8/15
From VIA
By Coffey N

NOTHING TO BE WRITTEN BY THE ADDRESSER ABOVE THIS LINE.

TO Lucknow Brigade

Sender's Number: Q1349
Day of Month: 7th
In reply to number: —
AAA

Final rendezvous for divisional supply column 8th instant will be usual offloading point for div troops supply column NORRENT FONTES at 2 pm aaa Brigade supply officers will take over their rations there.

FROM AA and QMG
1ST IND CAV DIVN
7.30 PM

App. 1

INSTRUCTIONS.

1. Telegrams in the field are accepted under the rulings in chapter XVI, F. S. R. II (Indian Supplement).

2. The addressor will enter (a) any instructions re the delivery of this message (e.g., "to await arrival") after the address in the space "Address TO," (b) the class of his message, following his signature, in space Z, e.g., "Clear line," "Urgent Railway," "Priority," "State," "Press Express," "Press," "Private Express," "Private."

3. If a receipt is required for the message it will be prepared by the addressor and signed by the Signaller in charge.

Gulab Singh & Sons, Calcutta.

MESSAGES, SIGNALS AND FIELD TELEGRAPHS.

Army Form C. 2121. Modified for India.

No. of Message 54

Prefix XB Code m.
Words. 23 Charge. (X) Stamps.
Recd. at 5.47
Date 8.3.15
From VIA

Office of Origin and Service Instructions.

VIA
Priority

Sent.
At
To
By

NOTHING TO BE WRITTEN BY THE ADDRESSER ABOVE THIS LINE.

TO Lucknow Bde

Sender's Number Q1355
Day of Month 8
In reply to number.
AAA

Supply Column can now offload and return to Railhead

6.15pm

FROM AA & QMG
1st Ind. Cav Div

Place
Time

INSTRUCTIONS.

1. Telegrams in the field are accepted under the rulings in chapter XVI, F. S. R. II (Indian Supplement).
2. The addressor will enter (a) any instructions re the delivery of this message (e.g., "to await arrival") after the address in the space "Address TO," (b) the class of his message, following his signature, in space Z, e.g., "Clear line," "Urgent Railway," "Priority," "State," "Press Express," "Press," "Private Express," "Private."
3. If a receipt is required for the message it will be prepared by the addressor and signed by the signaller in charge.

MESSAGES, SIGNALS AND FIELD TELEGRAPHS.

Army Form C. 2121. Modified for India.

Prefix	Code	m.	Words.	Charge.	(X)	For Stamps.	Recd. at	m.
Office of Origin and Service Instructions.			Sent. At m. To By				Date From By	

NOTHING TO BE WRITTEN BY THE ADDRESSOR ABOVE THIS LINE.

TO (SEE INSTRUCTIONS ON BACK.)	Lucknow Bde			

*Sender's Number.	Day of Month.	In reply to number.	AAA
Q 1362	8th		

final rendezvous nineth inst 2 pm AUCHY AUX BOIS cross roads except for divisional troops whose final rendezvous will be usual off loading point at FONTES

FROM	AA	and	QMG	1st
Place Time	Ind. 7.25	Cav pm	Div	

(Y) The above may be forwarded as now corrected. (Z) Class of Message.

Countersignature of Censor or Authorising Officer. | Signature of addressor and his instructions, vide reverse.

* This line should be erased if not required.

Appx B

INSTRUCTIONS.

1. Telegrams in the field are accepted under the rulings in chapter XVI, F. S. R. II (Indian Supplement).

2. The addressor will enter (a) any instructions re the delivery of this message (e.g., "to await arrival") after the address in the space "Address TO," (b) the class of his message, following his signature, in space Z, e.g., "Clear line," "Urgent Railway," "Priority," "State," "Press Express," "Press," "Private Express," "Private."

3. If a receipt is required for the message it will be prepared by the addressor and signed by the Signaller in charge.

MESSAGES, SIGNALS AND FIELD TELEGRAPHS.

Army Form C. 2121. Modified for India.

Prefix **2D** Code

Office of Origin and Service Instructions.

**PRIORITY
VIA**

Words. **37**

NOTHING TO BE WRITTEN BY THE ADDRESSOR ABOVE THIS LINE.

TO **RH BDE LUCKNOW**

Sender's Number: **Q 1373**   Day of Month: **9th**

Supply lorries can now ~~auto~~ unload except hay aaa old lorries except ~~to~~ hay lorries may leave off loading points and return to Railhead

(SC 241)

FROM: **AA AND QMG 1ST
IND CAV DIV**

INSTRUCTIONS.

1. Telegrams in the field are accepted under the rulings in chapter XVI, F. S. R. II (Indian Supplement).
2. The addressor will enter (a) any instructions re the delivery of this message (e.g., "to await arrival") after the address in the space "Address TO," (b) the class of his message, following his signature, in space Z, e.g., "Clear line," "Urgent Railway," "Priority," "State," "Press Express," "Press," "Private Express," "Private."
3. If a receipt is required for the message it will be prepared by the addressor and signed by the Signaller in charge.

Gulab Singh & Sons, Calcutta.

MESSAGES, SIGNALS AND FIELD TELEGRAPHS.

Army Form C. 2121. Modified for India.

TO: LUCKNOW BDE

Sender's Number: Q1374
Day of Month: 9th

May lorries on return offloading can to tow railhead point leave and

FROM: AA AND QMG
Place: 1ST IND CAV DIVN

apr 5

INSTRUCTIONS.

1. Telegrams in the field are accepted under the rulings in chapter XVI, F. S. R. II (Indian Supplement).

2. The addressor will enter (a) any instructions re the delivery of this message (e.g., "to await arrival") after the address in the space "Address TO," (b) the class of his message, following his signature, in space Z, e.g., "Clear line," "Urgent Railway," "Priority," "State," "Press Express," "Press," "Private Express," "Private."

3. If a receipt is required for the message it will be prepared by the addressor and signed by the Signaller in char

MESSAGES, SIGNALS AND FIELD TELEGRAPHS.

Army Form C. 2121. Modified for India.

No. of Message **9**

Prefix — Code — m. Words. **31** Charge. (X) For stamps. ● Recd. at **1028** m. Date **10-3-15** From **VIA** By **AA**

Office of Origin and Service Instructions.

VIA
2add.

Sent. At m. To By

NOTHING TO BE WRITTEN BY THE ADDRESSOR ABOVE THIS LINE.

TO: **Lucknow Bde**

Sender's Number: **41376** Day of Month: **10** In reply to number: AAA

Final RV today for supply column is AUCHY AU BOIS Cross roads at 2 pm

S.C. 245   10.3.15

Supply Officer
For information
GR ? ?

FROM: **AA & Q MG**
Place: **1st Ind Cav Div**
Time: **10.20 am**

appx 6

INSTRUCTIONS.

1. Telegrams in the field are accepted under the rulings in chapter XVI, F. S. R. II (Indian Supplement).
2. The addressor will enter (a) any instructions re the delivery of this message (e.g., "to await arrival") after the address in the space "Address TO," (b) the class of his message, following his signature, in space Z, e.g., "Clear line," "Urgent Railway," "Priority," "State," "Press Express," "Press," "Private Express," "Private."
3. If a receipt is required for the message it will be prepared by the addressor and signed by the Signaller in char

MESSAGES, SIGNALS AND FIELD TELEGRAPHS.

Army Form C. 2121. Modified for India.

TO Lucknow Bde

Sender's Number: Q 1385
Day of Month: 10

Supply lorries can leave the offloading points and return to railhead

FROM
Place: AA and QMG 1st
       and Cav Div
Time: 6.15

INSTRUCTIONS.

1. Telegrams in the field are accepted under the rulings in chapter XVI, F. S. R. II (Indian Supplement).

2. The addressor will enter (a) any instructions re the delivery of this message (e.g., "to await arrival") after the address in the space "Address TO," (b) the class of his message, following his signature, in space Z, e.g., "Clear line," "Urgent Railway," "Priority," "State," "Press Express," "Press," "Private Express," "Private."

3. If a receipt is required for the message it will be prepared by the addressor and signed by the Signaller in charge.

Gulab Singh & Sons, Calcutta-

Copy No 6

OPERATION ORDER NO 1.
By
Br: Gen. Fasken,
comdg;
Lucknow Cavalry Brigade.

10.3.1915

1. The Brigade will march tomorrow morning to the vicinity of MARLES, via FONTAINE-LEZ-HERMANS — HUMERVAL — PERNES — CAMBLAIN-CHATELAIN.
   Starting Point. NEDONCHELLE Church at 4.30 a.m.

2. Order of march as under :—

(a) A.G. (Name of Commander to be submitted at S.P.)
   1 Squadron. 29" Lancers.

Main Body:—
   29" Lancers (less 1 squadron)
   K.D.Gs.
   36" Jacob's Horse (less 2 troops.)
   2nd and 3rd chargers of whole Brigade.
   Regimental Reserve Ammunition

Rear Guard:—
   1 Troop 36" J.H.

(b). O.C. 36 J.H will detail 1 troop to report to Brigade Major at Starting Point. These men will be dropped en route for closing roads & will rejoin Rear Guard when the Brigade has passed.

3. A Echelon Transport (less Regimental Reserve Ammunition) under an Officer to be detailed by O.C. K.D.G. and B Echelon Transport, under 1 officer or

3. (continued)
Interpreters per Unit will each march in rear of Units — the whole under the Brigade Transport Officer. B ech Echelons will be in rear of the AMBALA Brigade and in front of the AMBALA Brigade Transport.

Head of A Echelon to be at Brigade Starting Point at 6.15 a.m.

K.D.G Transport will ensure that the FLECHIN – FEBVIN, LIGNY – FEBVIN, and FEBVIN – FONTAINE-LEZ-HERMANS roads are kept clear for the fighting portion of AMBALA Brigade to pass.

29' Lancers will similarly keep the FONTAINE-LEZ-HERMANS – AUMERVAL road clear.

4. Reports to head of Main Body.

10.20 p.m.

J. Thompson Capt
B Major

"A" Form.
Army Form C. 2121.

MESSAGES AND SIGNALS.

No. of Message

Prefix	Code	m.	Words	Charge			
Office of Origin and Service Instructions.					This message is on a/c of	Rec'd. at	m.
			Sent			Date	
			At	m.	Service.	V 11.III.15. 1A
			To			From	
			By		(Signature of "Franking Officer.")	By	

TO { Sialkot, Ambala, Lucknow } Bde

Sender's Number	Day of Month	In reply to Number	AAA
Q 1387	10th		

One hay lorry per unit will deliver tomorrow morning at final rendezvous X roads in LA BOEUVRIERE south of railway 8 a.m.

From: Anderson
Place: 1/2 C.S.
Time: 10.40 p.m.

The above may be forwarded as now corrected.

(Z) Col W.R. Birdwood Major

Censor. Signature of Addresser or person authorised to telegraph in his name

* This line should be erased if not required.
158 S. B. Ltd. Wt. W5673/619—50,000. 10/14. Forms C2121/10.

"A" Form.
Army Form 2121.

MESSAGES AND SIGNALS. No. of Message _____

Prefix ____ Code ____ m.	Words.	Charge.	This message is on a/c of	Recd. at ____ m.
Office of Origin and Service Instructions.	Sent			Date
Priority	At ____ m. To ____ By ____		Service ____ (Signature of "Franking Officer.")	From ____ By ____

TO { _____ / _____ / Sgt Roe } O/C Supply Col
O/C ASC

Sender's Number	Day of Month	In reply to Number	
Q 1388	11		AAA

As this many roads are road between CHOCQUES and MARLES are sadly blown right present via LILLERS BURBURE RAIMBERT AUCHEL to MARLES and between via LOZINGHEM and LILLERS aaa rendezvous will be 5 pm at South WEST end of MARLES where horse transport will right and Supply to ...

From: 7 Cav Div
Place:
Time: 1.35 pm

The above may be forwarded as now corrected. (Z) Lewis

Censor. Signature of Addressor or person authorised to telegraph in his name

* This line should be erased if not required.

"A" Form. Army Form
MESSAGES AND SIGNALS.
No. of Message

Prefix____ Code____ m. | Words | Charge | This message is on a/ | Recd. at____ m.
Office of Origin and Service Instructions. | Sent | | Service | Date____
Priority | At____ m. | | | From____
 | To____ | | |
 | By____ | | (Signature of "Franking Officer.") | By____

TO { SIALKOT
     AMBALA   } Cav Bde.
     LUCKNOW

Sender's Number: G.A. 162 | Day of Month: 12th | In reply to Number | AAA

Division will move into billets as follows :- AMBALA Bde will march to CAUCHY ALATOUR and FLORINGHEM via CALONNE-RICOUART at 11 a.m. and with its transport will be clear of turning to AUCHEL ¼ mile North West of 1st C of CALONNE-RICOUART by 1 pm. AAA LUCKNOW Bde will march at 12.30 pm. to AUCHEL via the turning above mentioned and with its transport will be clear of MARLES village by 2 pm. AAA SIALKOT Bde will not pass the L of LAPUGNOY till 1.45 pm. and will billet in MARLES AAA Final rendezvous for Supply Column is the north end of RAIMBERT at 3.0 pm.

From: 1st Ind Cav Div
Place:
Time: 9.50 a.m.

The above may be forwarded as now corrected. (Z) Sgd E Conway Gordon Major
Censor. Signature of Addresser or person authorised to telegraph in his name

SO 1st Ind Cav Div.

MESSAGES AND SIGNALS.

"A" Form.   Army Form C. 2121.

Prefix	Code	m.	Words.	Charge.	This message is on a/c of:	Recd. at	m.
Office of Origin and Service Instructions.			Sent		Service.	Date	
			At ___ m.			From	
			To			By	
			By		(Signature of "Franking Officer.)		

TO: Sialkot Anirala ?

Sender's Number	Day of Month	In reply to Number	AAA

SC 260 / Supplies

Recd 10-45 Am

From: ...
Place:
Time: 9.20 am

The above may be forwarded as now corrected.   (Z)

Censor.   Signature of Addressor or person authorised to telegraph in his name

* This line should be erased if not required.

MESSAGES, SIGNALS AND FIELD TELEGRAPHS.

Army Form C. 2121. Modified for India.

TO: LUCKNOW BDE

Sender's Number: A1410
Day of Month: 13

Lorries can now return to railhead. Please inform section officer of supply column that this also refers to lorries of divl troops

SC.266

4.45 pm
AMM

FROM: AA AND QMG
Place: 1ST IND CAV DIV
Time: 4.15 PM

INSTRUCTIONS.

1. Telegrams in the field are accepted under the rulings in chapter XVI, F. S. R. II (Indian Supplement).

2. The addressor will enter (a) any instructions *re* the delivery of this message (*e.g.*, "to await arrival") after the address in the space "Address TO," (b) the class of his message, following his signature, in space Z, *e.g.*, "Clear line," "Urgent Railway," "Priority," "State," "Press Express," "Press," "Private Express," "Private."

3. If a receipt is required for the message it will be prepared by the addressor and signed by the Signaller in charge.

MESSAGES, SIGNALS AND FIELD TELEGRAPHS.

Army Form C. 2121. Modified for India.   No. of Message 46

Prefix / M Code / -- m. Words 23 Charge. (X) Stamps. Recd. at 11·7 M m.
Office of Origin and Service Instructions.
VIA
Sent. At 11·10 P m. Date 14·3·15
To T.C. From VIA
By Austin By Austin

NOTHING TO BE WRITTEN BY THE ADDRESSER ABOVE THIS LINE.

TO: Lucknow
Ambala Beh?

Sender's Number: 2·4·15   Day of Month: 14   In reply to number.   AAA

Finals RV for supply column today north end of RAIMBERT 3 pm

Sc 267

Supplies
Q M General?
Capt
S Capt

FROM: M Ind Cav Div
Place:
Time: 10·86 AM

INSTRUCTIONS.

1. Telegrams in the field are accepted under the rulings in chapter XVI, F. S. R. II (Indian Supplement).
2. The addressor will enter (a) any instructions re the delivery of this message (e.g., "to await arrival") after the address in the space "Address TO," (b) the class of his message, following his signature, in space Z, e.g., "Clear line," "Urgent Railway," "Priority," "State," "Press Express," "Press," "Private Express," "Private."
3. If a receipt is required for the message it will be prepared by the addressor and signed by the Signaller in charge.

Gulab Singh & Sons, Calcutta.

MESSAGES, SIGNALS AND FIELD TELEGRAPHS.

Army Form C. 2121. Modified for India.

No. of Message 47

Prefix M Code LCA m.
Words: 19 Charge. (X) or Stamps.
Recd. 4 P.m. m.

Office of Origin and Service Instructions.
VIA
Sent. At ___ m.
To ___
By ___

Date P.14 14/3/15
From VIA
By Austen

NOTHING TO BE WRITTEN BY THE ADDRESSOR ABOVE THIS LINE.

TO { AMBALA Bdes
      Lucknow }

(SEE INSTRUCTIONS ON BACK.)

Sender's Number.	Day of Month.	In reply to number.	AAA
9/4/5	14th		

Cancel my 12/7 aaa Further orders with issue

LC.368

FROM 1st Ind Cav Div
Place
Time 11:15 AM

(Y) The above may be forwarded as now corrected. (Z) Class of Message.

Countersignature of Censor or Authorising Officer. Signature of addressor and his instructions, vide reverse.

* This line should be erased if not required.

INSTRUCTIONS.

1. Telegrams in the field are accepted under the rulings in chapter XVI, F. S. R. II (Indian Supplement).
2. The addressor will enter (a) any instructions re the delivery of this message (e.g., "to await arrival") after the address in the space "Address TO," (b) the class of his message, following his signature, in space Z, e.g., "Clear line," "Urgent Railway," "Priority," "State," "Press Express," "Press," "Private Express," "Private."
3. If a receipt is required for the message it will be prepared by the addressor and signed by the Signaller in charge.

Gulab Singh & Sons, Calcutta.

MESSAGES, SIGNALS AND FIELD TELEGRAPHS.

Army Form C. 2121. Modified for India.   No. of Message 50

Prefix_____ Code_____ m.   Words.   Charge.   (X)   or Stamps.   Recd. at_____ m.
Office of Origin and Service Instructions.   Date_____
                            Sent.
VIA   At_____ m.   From_____
                            To_____
                            By_____   By_____

NOTHING TO BE WRITTEN BY THE ADDRESSOR ABOVE THIS LINE.

TO: Ambala Bdes.
    Lucknow

Sender's Number	Day of Month	In reply to number	AAA
C.1419	14th		

Supply column will deliver early ~~tomorrow~~ morning instead of ~~today~~ RV will be notified later

14/3/05   Supply Officer Lucknow Bde
           Forwarded

           GP Maitland
           Staff Capt

FROM
Place: AA & QMG 1st 3rd Div
Time: 12.50 pm

INSTRUCTIONS.

1. Telegrams in the field are accepted under the rulings in chapter XVI, F. S. R. II (Indian Supplement).

2. The addressor will enter (a) any instructions re the delivery of this message (e.g., "to await arrival") after the address in the space "Address TO," (b) the class of his message, following his signature, in space Z, e.g., "Clear line," "Urgent Railway," "Priority," "State," "Press Express," "Press," "Private Express," "Private."

3. If a receipt is required for the message it will be prepared by the addressor and signed by the Signaller in charge.

MESSAGES, SIGNALS AND FIELD TELEGRAPHS.

Army Form C. 2121. Modified for India.

TO: Lucknow Bde

Sender's Number: 0423
Day of Month: 14th

Final RV Supply Column old off loading point have divisional troops at Torrent Fontes at 7AM 15th

FROM: 1st Ind Cav Div

INSTRUCTIONS.

1. Telegrams in the field are accepted under the rulings in chapter XVI, F. S. R. II (Indian Supplement).
2. The addressor will enter (a) any instructions re the delivery of this message (e.g., "to await arrival") after the address in the space "Address TO," (b) the class of his message, following his signature, in space Z, e.g., "Clear line," "Urgent Railway," "Priority," "State," "Press Express," "Press," "Private Express," "Private."
3. If a receipt is required for the message it will be prepared by the addressor and signed by the Signaller in charge.

Gulab Singh & Sons, Calcutta—

"A" Form. Army Form C. 2121.

MESSAGES AND SIGNALS.

No. of Message _____

Prefix ____ Code ____ m.	Words	Charge	This message is on a/c of:	Recd. at ____ m.
Office of Origin and Service Instructions.	Sent			Date ____
_____	At ____ m.		Service.	From ____
_____	To ____			By ____
	By ____		(Signature of "Franking Officer.")	

| TO { | K of 2 | 29: | Lan | 36. H |

| * Sender's Number | Day of Month | In reply to Number | AAA |
| BM 27 | 14 | | |

Transport of 38. will be marching
about 10 p.m. and the B. Bn
about 1 a.m. Orders are following

From: RD My
Place:
Time: 5.37 p.m.

The above may be forwarded as now corrected. (Z)

Censor. Signature of Addressor or person authorised to telegraph in his name

* This line should be erased if not required.

"A"-Form.   Army Form C. 2121.

MESSAGES AND SIGNALS.

TO	K D G 29 L 36 H

Sender's Number	Day of Month	In reply to Number	AAA
BM 46	17		

Billets are allotted this Bde H.Q. LONGHEM aaa 29 Lancers ESTREE BLANCHE and FLECHINELLE aaa 36 H LIETTRES and LINGHEM aaa KDG stand fast

From BM
Place
Time 6.30 pm

Serial No 244.

WAR DIARY

Supply Officer, Lucknow Cavalry Brigade, 1st Indian Cavalry Division.

February 1915 to 28th February 1915

Confidential

Army Form C. 2118.

Supply officer Lucknow Cavalry Bde
1st Indian Cavalry Division
I.E.F.A.

WAR DIARY or INTELLIGENCE SUMMARY.

(Erase heading not required)

Instructions regarding War Diaries and Intelligence Summaries are contained in F. S. Regs., Part II and the Staff Manual respectively. Title page will be prepared in manuscript.

Hour, Date, Place.	Summary of Events and Information	Remarks and references to Appendices.
HEUCHIN PAS-DE-CALAIS February 3rd 1915	Captain H.M. WHITTELL Sumd T. Corps assumed the duties of Brigade Supply officer vice Captain BELL MURRAY Sumd Corps transferred.	
February 6th 1915	French Interpreter EDMOND BRAUN 112th Infantry arrived for duty vice French Interpreter JACQUES ARDITI 3rd Infantry transferred.	
Feb 1st to 26th	Brigade remained in Billets as follows. Kings Dragoon Guards at LISBOURG. 36th Jacob's Horse at PREDEFIN 29th Lancers at FONTAINE Headquarters at HEUCHIN Daily Supply Routine duties carried out during this period	

No. 227
2.3.15.

HMWhittell Capt.
Bde. Supply Officer

Army Form C. 2118.

WAR DIARY
INTELLIGENCE SUMMARY
(Erase heading not required.)

Instructions regarding War Diaries and Intelligence Summaries are contained in F. S. Regs., Part II. and the Staff Manual respectively. Title pages will be prepared in manuscript.

Hour, Date, Place	Summary of Events and Information	Remarks and references to Appendices
1st January to 31st January 1915: MEERUT.	Carried on routine duties as usual. J.W. Sunny Captain. Brigade Supply Officer Lucknow Cavalry Brigade 1st Indian Cavalry Division	

244

WAR DIARY
OF
Brigade Supply Officer Lucknow Cavalry Brigade 1st Indian Cavalry Division

From 1st January 1915 To 31st January 1915

Serial No 244.

121/6/23

WAR DIARY
OF
Supply Officer Lucknow Cavalry Brigade

FROM 1st April 1915 TO 30th April 1915.

Confidential

April 1915

Brigade Supply Officer
Lucius Cavalry Brigade

WAR DIARY
or
INTELLIGENCE SUMMARY

Army Form C. 2118.

(Erase heading not required.)

Hour, Date, Place	Summary of Events and Information	Remarks and references to Appendices
ESTREE BLANCHE April 15	Brigade was in billets as follows.	
April 16	Headquarters LONGHEM.	
April 23rd	Kings Dragoon Guards FLESHIN, BONCOURT, CUHEM } Routine duty in billets	
	24th Lancers ESTREE BLANCHE, FLECHINELLE }	
	36th Jacobs Horse LIETTRES, LONGHEM }	
24.4.15 10.50 am	Brigade ordered to be in readiness to move at 2 hours notice	
12.30 am	Informed that Supply Lorries must not be unloaded but lorries having already left unloaded that required Groom supplies not required for immediate consumption by units were recalled and supplies reloaded	
6.10 pm	S.S.O. intimated final rendezvous for above lorries the at STAPLE at 9 pm	
7 pm	Brigade marched for ESTREE BLANCHE	
9 pm	Final Rendezvous of Lorries at STAPLE. Lorries for Brigade billeted area Rosano	

Confidential

Army Form C. 2118.

Instructions regarding War Diaries and Intelligence Summaries are contained in F.S. Regs., Part II. and the Staff Manual respectively. Title pages will be prepared in manuscript.

WAR DIARY
or
INTELLIGENCE SUMMARY.
(Erase heading not required.)

Hour, Date, Place	Summary of Events and Information	Remarks and references to Appendices
OXELAERE		
6pm 25.4.15	Borders arrived at final rendezvous at LONGUE CROIX and supplies delivered from G.S.	
6.10pm	Patrol reaches for a mount orders	
26.4.15 6pm	Borders arrived at final rendezvous as for yesterday. Borders returned pending orders	
9.15pm	Borders unloaded and returned to railhead. Orders for this received B.O. 9.15pm	
27.4.15	Rendezvous same time and place as yesterday	
ST. JANS TER BIEZEN	Orders received to march to ST JANSTERBIEZEN at 12.15pm	
	to billets rendezvous behind railway in Burgum and parked at—	
	ST. MARIE CAPPEL	
6pm	had lorries at final rendezvous at road junction South of	
	RATTEKOT INN 2 miles South of WATOU	
10.10pm	Lorries having finished by orders moved to Divisional Headquarters at two hours for their return to railhead	

Army Form C. 2118.

WAR DIARY
or
INTELLIGENCE SUMMARY.

(Erase heading not required.)

Instructions regarding War Diaries and Intelligence Summaries are contained in F.S. Regs., Part II. and the Staff Manual respectively. Title pages will be prepared in manuscript.

Hour, Date, Place	Summary of Events and Information	Remarks and references to Appendices
29.4.15	Rendezvous same measures place as yesterday at 5 p.m. Instructions issued that pending further orders lorries should be dismissed at 8.50 p.m. This was done.	
30.4.15	Rendezvous same place as yesterday at 4.30 p.m. Instructions issued that in absence of other orders lorries are to return to railhead at 9 p.m. This was done.	Armature Capt. Brigade Supply Officer Lucknow Cavalry Brigade

Land 244

121/6502

WAR DIARY
OF

Brigade Supply Officer, Lucknow Cavalry Brigade.

From 1st May 1915 to 31st May 1915.

Army Form C. 2118.

WAR DIARY
of Brigade Supply Officer
INTELLIGENCE SUMMARY. Lucknow Cavalry Brigade

(Erase heading not required.) 1.5.15 to 31.5.15

Hour, Date, Place	Summary of Events and Information	Remarks and references to Appendices
ST JAN TER BIEZEN 1.5.15	No change. Final Rendezvous for lorries same place as yesterday at 4.30 pm. Instructions issued that Brigade will return to its previous billeting area South of CASSEL tomorrow.	
2.5.15	Brigade marched to billeting area South of CASSEL and Mohnchives arrived its ready to move at 4 hours notice. Final Rendezvous for lorries at LURGE CROIX 5pm. Lorries returned breakfast at 9pm.	
3.5.15	No change	
4.5.15	Informer Brigade will move tomorrow to billeting area near MAMETZ	
5.5.15	Brigade moved to area notified yesterday. Final rendezvous for lorries 4pm AIRE	
6.5.15 to	No change. Routine duties to 15.5.15	
16.5.15		

Army Form C. 2118.

WAR DIARY
or
INTELLIGENCE SUMMARY.

(Erase heading not required.)

Instructions regarding War Diaries and Intelligence Summaries are contained in F.S. Regs., Part II. and the Staff Manual respectively. Title pages will be prepared in manuscript.

Hour, Date, Place		Summary of Events and Information	Remarks and references to Appendices
17.5.15	1.25 p.m.	Orders received that everything ready for a move. Brigade moves later to ALLOUAGNE. Brigade remaining in billets at MAMETZ.	
18.5.15	2.30 p.m.	Brigade moved into billets at BURBURE. Found rendezvous for Supply Column at South west corner of ALLOUAGNE at 3.45 p.m.	
19.5.15	1.30 p.m.	Brigade moved to original billeting area in MAMETZ. Final rendezvous for Brigade AIRE at 2.30 p.m. Bruno remained in billeting area until all ranks were cleared of troops moving in.	
20.5.15 & 25.5.15		No change.	
26.5.15		Informed that Division moves at 6.30 am tomorrow.	
27.5.15		Brigade moved to area near OXELAERE	
28.5.15		Brigade moved to L'IERNELSE RIDGE. Van diamonds run from each regiment ordered for YLAMATINGE and van truss handed over to Supply Officer Divisional Troops for rations.	
29.5.15 & 31.5.15		Final rendezvous for lorries for mounted troops at LA MENEGHAT 5 p.m. No change.	

(73989) W4441—463. 400,000. 9/14. H.&J.Ltd. Forms/C. 2118/10.

Hamilton Capt.
B.O. Kuchner Army Bde

Serial No 244.

12/6948

WAR DIARY OF

Supply Officer, Lucknow Cavalry Brigade.

FROM 1st August 1915 TO 31st August 1915

Confidential
5/9/26

Army Form C. 2118.

(Brigade Supply Officer
 Lucknow Cavalry Brigade
 I.E.F.A.

WAR DIARY
or
INTELLIGENCE SUMMARY.
(Erase heading not required.)

Instructions regarding War Diaries and Intelligence Summaries are contained in F.S. Regs., Part II. and the Staff Manual respectively. Title pages will be prepared in manuscript.

Hour, Date, Place	Summary of Events and Information	Remarks and references to Appendices
1. 8.15	Brigade marched at 11 am to FRUGES. 2 oclock sta with of the Brigade Hq Ist(Kings) Dragoon Guards, 29th Lancers, 36th (?) Horse and U Battery R.H.A the following units for divisional Troops were attached Field Squadron R.E. H.Q. Jat Ind. R.H.A. Bde H.Q. A.S.C. Lucknow Cavalry Field Ambulance H.Q. and 1 Sect. Divisional Ammunition Col. The Field Remount Section for Corps Troops were also attached. It carried rations for men and animals for four days except fodder which was supplied from supply Column. Units were billetted as follows Bde Hdqrs. 36th Horse U Battery R.H.A. HDQRS R.H.A HdQrs and Ist D.O.C. } FRUGES 29th Lancers Kings Dragoon Guards Field Ambulance H.Q. A.S.C. Final Rendezvous for Supply Column was at Cross road at DENNE BROEUCQ at 5 p.m.	Ref. MAP 1/80000 BLAN-ARRAS Appendix 1

A.G.S. OFFICE AT THE
No. 12314 C.
10 SEP 1915
INDIAN SECTION

Army Form C. 2118.

WAR DIARY
or
INTELLIGENCE SUMMARY.
(Erase heading not required.)

Instructions regarding War Diaries and Intelligence Summaries are contained in F.S. Regs., Part II. and the Staff Manual respectively. Title pages will be prepared in manuscript.

Hour, Date, Place	Summary of Events and Information	Remarks and references to Appendices
2.8.15	Brigade marched today to CORTES at 9 a.m. and on arrival were billeted as follows.	
	1st (King) Dragoon Guards } MARESQUEL Bde. Hdqrs.	
	36th Jacobs Horse ECQUINCOURT and part of AUBIN ST VAAST South of the railway	
	29th Lancers CORTES	
	All other units AUBIN ST VAAST.	
	Divisions for Supply Column was at the four cross roads at PONT ST MICHEL at 4 p.m.	AmmCol
3.8.15	Brigade marched in two columns at 5 and 7 am to meeting area South of ABBEVILLE - BERNAVILLE Road and on arrival were billeted as follows:-	
	Hdqrs. A.S.C. COULONVILLERS Hdqrs. R.H.A. MAISON - Rolland. Field Squadron. MESNIL - Domqueur Divisional Amm Col } LONGVILLERS Hdqrs L } S U Battery R.H.A. BEAUMETZ Kings Dragoon Guards DOMQUEUR 29th Lancers FRANSU 36th Jacobs Horse RIBEAUCOURT 9th Hdqrs HOUDENCOURT.	

Army Form C. 2118.

WAR DIARY
or
INTELLIGENCE SUMMARY.
(Erase heading not required.)

Instructions regarding War Diaries and Intelligence Summaries are contained in F.S. Regs., Part II. and the Staff Manual respectively. Title pages will be prepared in manuscript.

Hour, Date, Place	Summary of Events and Information	Remarks and references to Appendices
4. 8. 15	Rendezvous for Supply Column was at cross roads one mile south of YVRENCH at 4pm.	
	Brigade (1st Kings Dragoons, 30th Horse, 29th Lancers) was en route at 8am for Billeting area ST. LEGER les DOMART. All other troops left Rendezvous under orders for the Brigade or Divisional troops were billeted as follows.	
	1st Kings Dragoon Guards } ST. LEGER les DOMART 29th Lancers Brigade Headquarters } BERTEAUCOURT les DAMES 36th Jacobs Horse Rendezvous for Supply Column was at cross roads at junction S of SURCAMPS at 4pm	
5. 8. 15	Final Rendezvous for Supply Column was at cross roads in E - LONGPRE-les-Corps-Saints at 2.30 pm	Army Corps.
6. 8. 15	No change	
7. 8. 15	Billet was altered as follows: 29th Lancers MONTRELET and FIEFFES Bde. HdQrs CANAPLES Kings Dragoon Guards HALLOY-les-Pernois and PERNOIS 36th Jacobs Horse and MVS at BERTEAUCOURT les Dames	

Army Form C. 2118.

WAR DIARY
or
INTELLIGENCE SUMMARY.

(Erase heading not required.)

Instructions regarding War Diaries and Intelligence Summaries are contained in F.S. Regs., Part II. and the Staff Manual respectively. Title pages will be prepared in manuscript.

Hour, Date, Place	Summary of Events and Information	Remarks and references to Appendices
8.8.15 to 15.8.15	No change	Amm Capt.
16" to 19.8.15	No change	Amm Capt.
20.8.15	Orders received that Divis in will occupy and hold the trenches between AUTHUILLE and HAMEL and that the Brigade will march at 11pm on 22nd. Figures were supplied today for delivering on 22nd as follows: A. Permanent billets (details morning or all) B. For delivering at BEAUCOURT where horses etc will remain the night after leaving the new trenches at FORCEVILLE C. For party for trenches D. For A Echelon plus 2 GS wagons were repeated in Permanent billets delivered.	
21.8.15	Two days rations for Horse in Permanent billets delivered.	Amm Capt.
22.8.15	Brigade marched at 11pm. Rations at BEAUCOURT were dumped and divided among the three units on arrival, there being Supply Officer Ambulance Bde. Trench Party under superintendence of Supply officer Ambulance Bde. Sgt Harvey and Westmacott Somersetshire detached for duty with Trench Party	Amm Capt.
23.8.15 to 27.8.15	No change	Amm Capt.

Army Form C. 2118.

WAR DIARY
or
INTELLIGENCE SUMMARY.
(Erase heading not required.)

Instructions regarding War Diaries and Intelligence Summaries are contained in F.S. Regs., Part II. and the Staff Manual respectively. Title pages will be prepared in manuscript.

Hour, Date, Place	Summary of Events and Information	Remarks and references to Appendices
28.8.15	Bde Hdqrs Transferred to BERNEUIL	
29.8.15	No change	
30.8.15	Rations delivered at 10.30 am. This arrangement is to continue daily until further notice	

Armitage Capt.
B.S.O.
Lucknow Cavalry Brigade

Serial No. 244

Confidential.

131/7601

War Diary

of

- - - - - Supply-Officer Lucknow Cavalry Brigade - - - - -

FROM 1st September 1915. TO 30th September 1915.

Army Form C. 2118.

WAR DIARY
or
INTELLIGENCE SUMMARY.

Supply officer
between army Posts
I.E.F.A.

(Erase heading not required.)

Instructions regarding War Diaries and Intelligence Summaries are contained in F.S. Regs., Part II. and the Staff Manual respectively. Title pages will be prepared in manuscript.

Hour, Date, Place	Summary of Events and Information	Remarks and references to Appendices
1.9.15	Instruction received that Trench Party was to relieve on or near 2/3 September and move to billeting area ST G RATIEN - FRECHENCOURT.	
2.9.15	Horses for Trench Party despatched from permanent billets at approx to near Trench party in relief. Trench Party returned to billeting areas on arrival yesterday and were sits allotted as follows — Hump Station from the Mobile Veterinary Section } ST G RATIEN 20th Lancers 36th Jacob's Horse } FRECHENCOURT.	Army Capt.
(blank)	Rations above were drawn up at 5 pm and left in charge of permanent supply officers.	Army Capt.
3.9.15	The parties who had out horses yesterday for Trench Party returned to permanent billets with other details in addition.	Army Capt. Army Capt.
4.9.15 to 6.9.15	No Change	

Army Form C. 2118.

WAR DIARY
or
INTELLIGENCE SUMMARY.
(Erase heading not required.)

Instructions regarding War Diaries and Intelligence Summaries are contained in F. S. Regs., Part II. and the Staff Manual respectively. Title pages will be prepared in manuscript.

Hour, Date, Place	Summary of Events and Information	Remarks and references to Appendices
9.9.15	Tree of Pinks which had been renamed "Digging Party" with the exception of 111 Sappers and 20 horse holders per regiment returned to Permanent Billets. Instructions received from S.S.O. that in future alterations in establishment involving 5/ men not to notified to Supply Officer. Supply Column Echelon after submission of daily returns.	Munro Capt.
10.9.15	Orders received that the Division will relieve the 2nd & 3rd Cav. Divs. in the trenches on the night of 12/13th September. Division with return for Ammunition on 13 horses to Billets at 4 p.m. Rations for party remaining in Billets were rail and one Division returned to railhead at Gorbecourt. Project marched at 8 p.m. to area ST GRATIEN - FRÉCHENCOURT.	Munro Capt.
11.9.15		Munro Capt.
12.9.15	No change	Munro Capt.
13.9.15	Red horses returned to permanent Billets.	Munro Capt.
14.9.15	Orders received that the Division will be relieved in the trenches on the night of 16/17th Sept.	
15.9.15	On a addition to the normal issue of rations at 10.30 a.m. (for ensuing day tomorrow) rations for consumption on 17th am and at 3.30 pm Ration for the men crossing to permanent billets while Transport Parties	

Army Form C. 2118.

WAR DIARY
or
INTELLIGENCE SUMMARY.
(Erase heading not required.)

Instructions regarding War Diaries and Intelligence Summaries are contained in F.S. Regs., Part II. and the Staff Manual respectively. Title pages will be prepared in manuscript.

Hour, Date, Place	Summary of Events and Information	Remarks and references to Appendices
16.9.15	relief is taking place wire removed and ammunition (for old horse party) was left in lorries and returned to rail head is to taken in and dumped at BEAUCOURT tomorrow. Red horse party marched at 1.0 p.m.	
17.9.15	unchanged	
18.9.15	Bombardment Brigade returned to permanent billets from town of Chuly in Trenches. Details of normal strength to etc. as per attached Statement. Compiled and circulated to other supply Officers. This is to be ready reference when Transport of units occur or when A or B Echelon is reached elsewhere from fighting troops."	" do
19.9.15	Instructions received that ration limit will be at 3 pm from tomorrow inclusive	Hon Dep. Remin Dep.
20.9.15	No change	
21.9.15	No change	

Army Form C. 2118.

WAR DIARY
or
INTELLIGENCE SUMMARY.
(Erase heading not required.)

Instructions regarding War Diaries and Intelligence Summaries are contained in F.S. Regs., Part II. and the Staff Manual respectively. Title pages will be prepared in manuscript.

Hour, Date, Place	Summary of Events and Information	Remarks and references to Appendices
22.9.15.	B Section wagons, after kits were dumped, were despatched to railhead where they were loaded with 2 days Iron Rations for British and Indian and 2 days Grain @ 9 lbs per animal. They now form the Brigade Section of Divisional Train and are under orders of O.C.D.C. under whom 2 days Iron rations for men form Reserve Pack Supply carried on pack animals.	Humphries Capt.
23.9.15	Brigade Section of Train moved to OBOGNE. E.S. Sgt Harvey in charge of Supplies on No 2 Section and Asst Bednon Lcl Cpl Supplies on No 1 Section. Sgt Harvey in relieving charge of Sections.	Humphries Capt.
24.9.15 to 30.9.15	} no change	Humphries Capt.

Humphries Capt.
PSSO.
Lucknow Cavalry Bde.

SERIAL NO. 244.

Confidential

War Diary

of

Supply Officer, Lucknow Cavalry Brigade.

FROM 1st October 1915 TO 31st December 1915

Army Form C. 2118.

WAR DIARY
or
INTELLIGENCE SUMMARY.
(Erase heading not required.)

Supply officer
Rickham Cavalry Bde

Instructions regarding War Diaries and Intelligence Summaries are contained in F. S. Regs., Part II. and the Staff Manual respectively. Title pages will be prepared in manuscript.

Hour, Date, Place	Summary of Events and Information	Remarks and references to Appendices
10.10.15	Informed that until further notice the Brigade will be ready to move at 10 hours notice	

WAR DIARY
or
INTELLIGENCE SUMMARY.

(Erase heading not required.)

Army Form C. 2118.

Instructions regarding War Diaries and Intelligence Summaries are contained in F. S. Regs., Part II. and the Staff Manual respectively. Title pages will be prepared in manuscript.

Hour, Date, Place	Summary of Events and Information	Remarks and references to Appendices
13. 10. 15	A readjustment of billeting areas took place today. The Brigade being now distributed as follows.	
	Headquarters MONTPLAISIR	
	M.V.S. ⎫	
	N.D.G. ⎬ LE QUESNEL FARM.	
	3d H. ⎭	
	Brigade Supply ⎫ BERMAVILLE	
	5 Y.O. ⎭	
	29 H. R.H.A. C.D.O. BOISBERGUES (Hd. qrs and 3 Squadrons)	
	U BATTERY R.H.A. ⎫ AUTHEUX	
	1 Section 2.4 Division ⎭	
	Rations for units not usual were distributed at 2 p.m. and for those marked as follows.	
	4 p.m.	
	Supply Co. issued rations in rear distribute as follows.	
	IYC0 ⎫ at Bde Supply IYC0 ⎫ at Bde Supply for 1 pont 1 pont ⎫ at Bde Hdqrs	
	I Ywghuann ⎭ I pont ⎭ Brit. Town or 1 Curative ⎭	
	I Ywghuann Officers	
14. 10. 15	No change. One Supply let Post ⎫ issues for Ordnance	
	1 pont posts ⎬	
	1 Knife R.A.S.C. ⎭	
	1 chopper	
	Instructions received that aux. M.T. Coy is to be split up into detachments which will be attached to Brigades of Infantry.	

WAR DIARY
or
INTELLIGENCE SUMMARY.
(Erase heading not required.)

Army Form C. 2118.

Hour, Date, Place	Summary of Events and Information	Remarks and references to Appendices
15.10.15	No change. Informed today that certain G.S. wagons with personnel and animals are to be attached from Aux. H.T. Company to Brigade Section of Divis'nal Train.) arranged with Supply Column that as to Aux. H.T. Coy. have hitherto been drawing their rations at railhead this practice will continue with the detachment attached to this Brigade and that in addition the rations for the Bde. Sect. Div'l Train will be also drawn at railhead. Visited the Bde. Sect. Div'l Train and directed him to draw 2 days supplies tomorrow for detachment arriving from Aux. instructed Sgt Harvey as above and directed him to draw H.T.Coy. as by drawing direct from Railhead they have been drawing one day and consuming the next, whereas with the rations brought out to troops on lorries they have been delivered on day and consumed the next (i.e. in 3rd day) hence the Aux H. T. Coy. has been consuming one day earlier. Received a report that a large percentage of tobacco had been received opened. Reported the matter personally to B.S.O. but was informed later by Echelon Supply Officer that the tins had been opened out the spot no reports had been made that had been opened out the spot no reports had been forced and derived Captain Flasco	

Army Form C. 2118.

Instructions regarding War Diaries and Intelligence Summaries are contained in F.S. Regs., Part II. and the Staff Manual respectively. Title pages will be prepared in manuscript.

WAR DIARY
or
INTELLIGENCE SUMMARY.
(Erase heading not required.)

Hour, Date, Place	Summary of Events and Information	Remarks and references to Appendices
	B.T.O. having proceeded today on 7 days temporary leave his duties devolve upon me.	
	From today the running room for supply column will be 11 am at FIENVILLERS. Promised that P&O men will attempt but must send a representative. Invited Sgt. Butterworth to undertake this duty in future has proposed a Hdqrs Lorry, supervise the work of Hdqrs and return to BERNAVILLE in completion. Attended the undermns personally today & see that Sgt. Butterworth understood his duties.	
16·10·15	Promised that the fatigue detailed for cook duty at railhead should be increased to 15 men. This will be arranged by Staff Captain on its arrival here from QA.I.O.W.C on return. Staff Captain informs me that he has received orders to cancel outfits of cool fatigue. The SSO will be asked to this no did 3rd.Aux Donnwood Train informed that no carts had arrived at OCCOCHES from Aux H.T.Coy. So asked no railhead and arranged for return for Bde Sect BSs loaded as usual on lorries for delivery tomorrow. Went to Bernard and saw S.S.O. who explained that the coal fatigue has be furnished by another Brigade. He supposed	

(73989) W4141-463. 400,000. 9/14. H.&J.Ltd. Forms/C.2118/10.

Army Form C. 2118.

WAR DIARY
or
INTELLIGENCE SUMMARY.
(Erase heading not required.)

Instructions regarding War Diaries and Intelligence Summaries are contained in F.S. Regs., Part II. and the Staff Manual respectively. Title pages will be prepared in manuscript.

Hour, Date, Place	Summary of Events and Information	Remarks and references to Appendices
	10 mail-bags lots of 10 Dungarees Suitings which had been issued to Cook Future of 29th Lancers on 10th and then disappeared.	
	Proceeded to 29th L. and had the Defaulter who was in charge	
	on that day produced. He stated that he had handed the Suitings	
	over to Agent Behari Lal. On Interview Behari Lal at once admits	
	He says the Suitings were handed over to the Corporal of the	
	Supply Column who was in charge of the Cook Group. Inspector	
	He wires to O.C. Supply Column at Finvillers.	
20.10.15	Informed Hd. Qrs. we will move to new Billetting area on	
28.10.15		
22.10.15	O/C moved into new Billetting areas as follows:—	
	29th Lancers ⎱ PICQUIGNY	
	Lucknow Am. F. Amb. ⎰ ST PIERRE A GOUY	
	36 Jacob's Horse LEMESGE, RIENCOURT, OISSY (Regtl. Hdqrs)	
	K.D.G. MOLLIENS-VIDAMES (Hdqrs), CAMPS.	
	BDE HDQRS + MVS CAVILLON	
	U Battery R.H.A. FOURDRINOY	

Army Form C. 2118.

WAR DIARY
or
INTELLIGENCE SUMMARY.
(Erase heading not required.)

Instructions regarding War Diaries and Intelligence Summaries are contained in F. S. Regs., Part II. and the Staff Manual respectively. Title pages will be prepared in manuscript.

Hour, Date, Place	Summary of Events and Information	Remarks and references to Appendices
23.10.15	Rendezvous for Supply Column Lorries was at 2.30 pm on the road between La Cencé Bridge PICQUIGNY and LA CHAUSSÉE. Rendezvous today same time and place as yesterday.	
26.10.15	Captain Wright R.T.O. evacuated sick today, his duties devolving upon me. Sgt. Hunney S.T.S. sent for duty to rail head in connection with receipt and dispatch of coal.	

WAR DIARY
INTELLIGENCE SUMMARY.
(Erase heading not required.)

Army Form C. 2118.

Hour, Date, Place	Summary of Events and Information	Remarks and references to Appendices
1.11.15	)	
to	} no change.	
5.11.15	)	
6.11.15	No 54/14363 Private NUTTALL (HARRY) joined as Clerk vice the Indian clerk who is to be despatched to the base on 15th inst. Work is continued in this area from the forest (BOIS DE CAYILLON). The french troops who previously occupied the area cut props for the trenches and the branches lying in the forest are worth by us as firewood. No charge is made except 2 francs on each cart-load taken away for fixed ones.	Ammr Capt-
8.11.15	The Mules received by 20th Lancers were deficient by 10 Cbs and were poor in quality 760 out of 35 being entirely fut. The mech was sent time 9 taken on 9 shewn a Petroleum Supply Officer who will complete the deficiency in the morning. The mules was then returned to 20th Lancers. Transport of V Battery R.H.A. inspected by me as Officiating B.T.O. many components are missing for the Curl the O.C. stating that they are not carried as they are available in firm equipment.	Ammr Capt-

Army Form C. 2118.

WAR DIARY
or
INTELLIGENCE SUMMARY.
(Erase heading not required.)

Instructions regarding War Diaries and Intelligence Summaries are contained in F.S. Regs., Part II. and the Staff Manual respectively. Title pages will be prepared in manuscript.

Hour, Date, Place	Summary of Events and Information	Remarks and references to Appendices
10. 11.15	S.S.O. asks for figures for horses forming Trench Party. If party is doing a tour of trench duty. Also sent him and to Echelon Supply officer. Rejiments asked to send in their figures by 9 am tomorrow	
11. 11.15	Figures received from 29th Lancers only. U Battery RHA informed me that they have received no instructions to despatch of any party so am waiting to submit figures. Telephoned in evening to K.D.G. and 36 H for figures. 36 H despatches figures which reached me this evening but K.D.G. replies want to submit today as reference to their horses to Bell Majors	
12. 11.15	Visited K.D.G. and obtained personnel figures and submitted statement to SSO and copies to Echelon Officers	
13. 11.15	Staff Captain states that a copy of S.R. 03 will be available for supply officer and first copy received today. So far no G.R.O.s have had to be borrowed from Pod. office which has not always been convenient as reference have constantly had to be made to G.R.O.s affecting units matters. Informed S.S.O. that as a rule no movement of Greeting Army appears to the movement a statement of requirements of stores for bedding for men will be submitted after arrival in new winter area of stores required daily	

WAR DIARY
or
INTELLIGENCE SUMMARY.
(Erase heading not required.)

Army Form C. 2118.

Hour, Date, Place	Summary of Events and Information	Remarks and references to Appendices
15.11.15	Mr Lieut. E.M. Elliot A.S.C. reported his arrival on appointment as Brigade Transport officer. Information received that Brigade will take up another area for billets. Men were visited by Requisitioning Officer and self. Issue of straw for bedding for horses stopped from today. AIYAR	
16.11.15	Sub Cond. C. NARAYANASAWMI despatched to Base. Instructions received that when personnel are despatched to Marseilles they should be provided with M.B. 63 for 5 days rations which should be delivered to Railway Supply Officer for compliance.	Aum Capt
Aum Capt
18.11.15	Staff Sgt. Newman S.T.C. joined the Brigade on transfer from Indian Base. Brigade moved into new billets as follows:— King's Dragoon Guards — LONGPRE 29th Lancers — CONDÉ FOLIE U Battery R.H.A. — BETTENCOURT VIEULAINE Bde. Hdqrs. 36th Jacob's Horse — FONTAINE, WANEL and SOREL LUCKNOW Field Amb. } FONTAINE Supply Hdqrs	Aum Capt

Army Form C. 2118.

WAR DIARY
or
INTELLIGENCE SUMMARY.

(Erase heading not required.)

Instructions regarding War Diaries and Intelligence Summaries are contained in F. S. Regs., Part II. and the Staff Manual respectively. Title pages will be prepared in manuscript.

Hour, Date, Place	Summary of Events and Information	Remarks and references to Appendices
19. 11. 15	⎫	
	⎬ no change.	
30. 11. 15	⎭	

Army Form C. 2118.

WAR DIARY
or
INTELLIGENCE SUMMARY.

(Erase heading not required.)

Supply Officer Lucknow Cavalry Brigade

Hour, Date, Place	Summary of Events and Information	Remarks and references to Appendices
13.12.15	Brigade being under orders to move to a new bivouacking area and as certain French stores were being sent in advance the three G.S. wagon loads of reserve rations were also sent in advance and dumped under a guard at the new Brigade H.Qrs.	
14.12.15	Two days rations ie for 15th and 16th were delivered to units. As Brigade is to move on 16th reguments were in doubt as to whether they can carry rations of 16th. Ammunition arose auricles that 2 grain rations and hay to extent forwhich it cannot be carried before marching off on 16th should be left in lorries. Lorries however through a misunderstanding chief not take balances.	
15.12.15	Regiments did did send to Fontaine supplies which they cannot carry. 29th Lancers sent in 39 bales hay. Nothing else sent by units. 29L divided issued back on 17th for the hay.	
16.12.15	Brigade marched to new bivouacking area as follows.	

Army Form C. 2118.

WAR DIARY
or
INTELLIGENCE SUMMARY.
(Erase heading not required.)

Instructions regarding War Diaries and Intelligence Summaries are contained in F.S. Regs., Part II. and the Staff Manual respectively. Title pages will be prepared in manuscript.

Hour, Date, Place	Summary of Events and Information	Remarks and references to Appendices
	Bde. Hdqrs. 36th Jacobs Horse } FRANLIEU K.P. Grenade QUESNOY 29th Lancers SAIGNEVILLE - GOUY M.V. Section. F	
	Received Field Ambulance firing out of the area and coming under supply charge of S.O. Divl. Troops.	
	Ascertainty that on the march 29 Lancers carried no hay in hay nets. Had they done so there was no necessity to dump any in old Billets. Matter approx to Staff Captain. Rations for 17th delivered in new area about 3pm.	
17.12.15	2 days rations delivered K.K.D.G. and 29L to relieve supplies; 1 day's to other units.	
18.12.15	A car sent by SSO for duty finishing return of supply car from workshops.	
19.12.15	2 days rations delivered to all units.	

Army Form C. 2118.

WAR DIARY
INTELLIGENCE SUMMARY.
(Erase heading not required.)

Instructions regarding War Diaries and Intelligence Summaries are contained in F.S. Regs., Part II. and the Staff Manual respectively. Title pages will be prepared in manuscript.

Hour, Date, Place	Summary of Events and Information	Remarks and references to Appendices
	The supply of firewood is likely to be difficult in its present area as the cutting down of supply if can be from mielland by one half necessitates purchase of a large quantity of firewood daily. The requisitioning office drew four O.S. wagon loads firewood from Octavia at Fosseine on 17th as wood arriving on 18th. The stocks in villages in this area are few and only sufficient for a few days supply. R.O. has heard that wood is obtainable from Forêt l'Abbaye and I noticed arrive where there is a forest, the owner however being away.	
20.12.15	R.O. arranged with owner of Forêt l'Abbaye for supply daily of 4500 K. cutwood @ 30 fr per 1000 K. He notices Forest. There is not much cut wood at present and it remains to be seen whether cutters will keep pace with our requirements. First supply to start tomorrow.	
21.12.15		
31.12.15	Rations daily in fields. Fuel is supplied unless arrangements of S.S.O. any Shortage is supplied by local purchase or from stores held by So Sint Troops	

Amitruue Capt
R.T.O.

SERIAL NO. 244

Confidential
War Diary
of

Supply Officer, Lucknow Cavalry Brigade.

FROM 1st January 1916. TO 31st January 1916.

Confidential

Brigade Supply Officer
Lucknow Cavalry Brigade
I.E.F.A.

47

WAR DIARY or INTELLIGENCE SUMMARY.

Army Form C. 2118.

(Erase heading not required.)

1 Div

Hour, Date, Place	Summary of Events and Information	Remarks and references to Appendices
1.1.16	} no change	
to 3.1.16		
4.1.16.	2800 kilos firewood purchased by us at COMPAGNIE weekly since of bedding for men at Bde. Hqtrs. made. G.O.C. decided that R.O. should ascertain the duties of Cavmo officer for the Brigade.	
7.1.16.	6 trapas despatched to draw wood from R.O. Civil Troops. 8000 kilos wood received but quality inferior being young and green.	
8.1.16	Reported that from the 12th inst. inclusive hay @ 6/- per arrived mg will be sent up from railhead & balance of ration must be purchased locally and that in addition a reserve up to 120 lbs per animal must be laid in as per an provide in bales of hay.	

Army Form C. 2118.

Instructions regarding War Diaries and Intelligence Summaries are contained in F.S. Regs., Part II. and the Staff Manual respectively. Title pages will be prepared in manuscript.

WAR DIARY
or
INTELLIGENCE SUMMARY.
(Erase heading not required.)

Hour, Date, Place	Summary of Events and Information	Remarks and references to Appendices
9.1.16.	5000 lbs baled hay issued and stored	
10.1.16.	Hay arrived today @ 6 lbs only instead of two arrangement. Starting from 12" = 7885 lbs stores 492# lbs potatoes and 10192 lbs issued purchased and stored. 29# Lancers in thes pol Fodder 2·3 Upton horse today.	
11.1.16.	11142 lbs baled hay stored 3872 lbs potatoes purchased and stored	
12.1.16	10192 lbs baled hay stored. Reported to R.S.O. that 40000 lbs baled hay on 19 lbs per horse have already been stored that total supplies instead of 180000 lbs at 90 lbs per horse have been arranged for. This will result in 130000 lbs. 3000 lbs per horse baled hay being in reserve by 20/=. Hence front placed over hay reserve. 12960 lbs baled hay placed to Reserve. Visited OCHANCOURT	
13.1.16.	9 had a reconnaissance for supplies carried out. 50000 lbs hay secured in the morning. 10500 lbs wood purchased and brought in.	

WAR DIARY
or
INTELLIGENCE SUMMARY.
(Erase heading not required.)

Army Form C. 2118.

Hour, Date, Place	Summary of Events and Information	Remarks and references to Appendices
14. 1. 16.	Hay for all units delivered and stored in FRAMLEU. Learned that 17th Lancers of Siellur Bde were purchasing fodder ie on its pen ie of this Bde. Seen from Siellur Bde. Delivered 650 Siellur Bde who directed in prevent receipt that purchases 64000 lbs Baled hay in reserve i.e. 30 lbs per animal	
15. 1. 16.	no change. Hay delivered and stored in FRAMLEU	
16. 1. 16.	Informed Supply Column to deliver hay to dump at CHEPY-YALINES railway station until further notice.	
17. 1. 16.	6 GS wagons obtained on loan from A.H. Transport Company and fire wood firewood brought into FRAMLEU from Grand Bois de CAHON. KDG commenced having oats crushed. Reported H30 in reply to a query that Issue Ration milk is refused by troops who have no complaints to our Colamp powers. Informed all units that certificates that vaccination are complete should reach us by noon on Saturdays	Dunn Capt.
18. 1. 16.		

Army Form C. 2118.

WAR DIARY
or
INTELLIGENCE SUMMARY.
(Erase heading not required.)

Instructions regarding War Diaries and Intelligence Summaries are contained in F.S. Regs., Part II. and the Staff Manual respectively. Title pages will be prepared in manuscript.

Hour, Date, Place	Summary of Events and Information	Remarks and references to Appendices
18.1.16.	115,600 lb baled hay @ 53½ ch per annum in reserve.	
20.1.16.	Reported to 950 that 6 Bicycles are on charge and are in loan with OC 2 QWC Replies to 950 in reply for enemy that no 2 saddle regiment put take roll direct fruit ration is being replaced and fresh known a surplus at the base no other unit desires a change.	
23.1.16	83 lb fodder per animal in reserve. Asked 950 whether Buscan cakes which can be purchased in Ablanville at 36 francs per 100 kilos may be issued to 29th Runcees in lieu of a proportion of oats.	
25.1.16	207,300 lb baled hay @ 9.5 ch per animal in reserve	
27.1.16	215,779 lb baled hay 3061 lb potatoes 350 MH lb were in reserve	

WAR DIARY
or
INTELLIGENCE SUMMARY.

(Erase heading not required.)

Army Form C. 2118.

Instructions regarding War Diaries and Intelligence Summaries are contained in F.S. Regs., Part II and the Staff Manual respectively. Title pages will be prepared in manuscript.

Hour, Date, Place	Summary of Events and Information	Remarks and references to Appendices
29.1.16.	Staff Sergeant Newman left for MONDICOURT to take over supply charge of a working party proceeding there from 2nd Corps tomorrow. Neophanan Soldier sn. sent with him.	
30.1.16.	Hay for Poor Helerp and one Indian regt. sent to CHEPY. YATIMES. Remainder delivered to units. Found 14% short. Found have been withdrawn to reprovision to our area but that we may continue period notifying they may not requisition without authority from him. Situation is not satisfactory as it would appear periodic shortages mean that conditions.	
31.1.16.	Hay from railhead delivered to units and no more will be sent to dump at CHEPY. YATIMES. 50 horses from each regiment were today attached to Canadian Cavalry Brigade. Rations were however delivered officially for those and regiments have been instructed to maintain on days rations for the 50 horses in case of sudden return. Indication was given that the receipt of 125 lbs baled hay per animal daily be given that the receipt... Reported to SSO that the receipt of 125 lbs baled hay per animal. Is now complete in this brigade. French authorities proclaimed through the town that all supplies are required for 10th French Corps and nothing is to be sold to the British. Matter reported to SSO as am now unable to purchase fodder locally and may have to use supply of baled hay we have in reserve for...	[signature] SSO Capt [illegible]

SERIAL No. 244

Confidential

War Diary

of

Supply Officer, Lucknow Cavalry Brigade.

FROM 1st February 1916 TO 29th February 1916

70

Confidential   Army Form C. 2118.

Brigade Supply Officer
Reserve Cavalry Brigade 1EFA

WAR DIARY
or
INTELLIGENCE SUMMARY.
(Erase heading not required.)

Instructions regarding War Diaries and Intelligence
Summaries are contained in F. S. Regs., Part II.
and the Staff Manual respectively. Title pages
will be prepared in manuscript.

Hour, Date, Place	Summary of Events and Information	Remarks and references to Appendices
1. 2. 16.	nothing to record	Brown Capt.
2. 2. 16		
3. 2. 16.	Informed that U Battery R.H.A. will arrive at OCHANCOURT on 5th and will require rations for next day. Telephoned to Supply Coy. Enquires as they stood in Battery Rowing area & Telephoned Battery for correct figures.	Brown Capt.
4. 2. 16	nothing to record	Brown Capt.
10.		
11. 2. 16		
12. 2. 16.	30 SK Meykmann Kandhai } joined from Base. 864 LN Meykmann Khairati	Brown Capt.
13. 2. 16.	nothing to record	Brown Capt.
14. 2. 16.	Temporary Tresonner Behari Lat found dead in his billet at 7am this morning. Death evidently due to suffocation, through sleeping in a closed room with a burning brazier of coal	Brown Capt.

WAR DIARY
or
INTELLIGENCE SUMMARY.
(Erase heading not required.)

Army Form C. 2118.

Hour, Date, Place	Summary of Events and Information	Remarks and references to Appendices
23.2.16	Kings Dragoon Guards asked for 2 tons Straw as Bedding for men. They cannot purchase it locally.	
24.2.16	Asked S.S.O. how our supply of 2 tons straw for K.D.G. Intimated that I am unable to purchase locally and as our consider a requisition would be accepted by Ingres who have already requisitioned from French Army in hand covering all stocks approved available. S.S.O. replied that he had asked Austin Engineer respecting same inform me later.	
2/6	Two days rations delivered to units today in view of prolonging Sat in.	
25.2.16	Lorries delivered one days supplies to all units in trucks. Arranged for 8 carts from Aux H.T. Company to draw water at el-CAHON and carts did not arrive, the N.C.O. in charge certified that he had been made spl. along some of roads 3rd Class Capart Maghal Abrim joined from Men. Pier Temp Pressmen Rations left (all receive)	
26.2.16	Lorries delivered one days supplies to units. Informed S.P.O. that Rescue Supply party moves to return in 27th as hour of arrival given.	

WAR DIARY
or
INTELLIGENCE SUMMARY.

Army Form C. 2118.

(Erase heading not required.)

Hour, Date, Place	Summary of Events and Information	Remarks and references to Appendices
26.2.16.	Asked S.S.O. to address French authorities to sanction purchase of being inoes in this area.	Wynn Capt
27.2.16.	P.S.O. Sector Bde informes us that it is unable to supply us with straw for bedding.	Wynn Capt
28.2.16	Owing to Thaw rations were brought to a central point for all Bdes & wagons & horses relieved & taken. Wagons brought in to unit. No hay was drawn, requirements of units being met from 3 day's reserve in hand at Hamelin	
29.2.16.	Rations received from Thaw Scheme 3 Sgt Human returned from duty with 37th Divn. Am.	
1.3.16	Rations received from Thaw Scheme	
2.3.16	Rations received from Thaw Scheme	
3.3.16	Rations received from Thaw Scheme. Informed that rations will not be drawn tomorrow and that manual lifting arrangements. Auctions are resumed on 4.3.16.	Wynn Little Capt OC Auctions Amm Park

SERIAL NO. 244

Confidential

War Diary

of

Supply Officer, Lucknow Cavalry Brigade

FROM 1st March 1916

TO 31st March 1916.

Confidential

Army Form C. 2118.

WAR DIARY
or
INTELLIGENCE SUMMARY.

Empire Supply Officer Lucknow Cavalry Bde.

(Erase heading not required.)

Instructions regarding War Diaries and Intelligence Summaries are contained in F. S. Regs., Part II. and the Staff Manual respectively. Title pages will be prepared in manuscript.

Hour, Date, Place	Summary of Events and Information	Remarks and references to Appendices
4.3.16.		
11.3.16.	3rd Class Agent Mag ful Alim evacuated to hospital. 3 Cart loads wood received.	
12.3.16.	One cart load wood received.	
22.3.16.	Captain A.S.C. took over duties of Brigade Supply Officer, Lucknow Cavalry Bde. from Captain Whitett.	Junior Capt.
25/3/16.	Orders received for move of Lucknow Br. Hd. Qrs to new area on 25th inst. Accompanied head transport to new area, to make	

(73989) W4141—463. 400,000. 9/14. H.&J.Ltd. Forms/C. 2118/10.

Army Form C. 2118.

WAR DIARY
or
INTELLIGENCE SUMMARY.

(Erase heading not required.)

Instructions regarding War Diaries and Intelligence Summaries are contained in F.S. Regs., Part II. and the Staff Manual respectively. Title pages will be prepared in manuscript.

Hour, Date, Place	Summary of Events and Information	Remarks and references to Appendices
25/3/16	Arrangements for wood chopping in west billets. Returned some evening to FRANEU, leaving field Tons — ford in west area. Received orders (verbally) move on 25th. Changing date to 26th. Went up to west area with Bgr Pennew.	
26/3/16	Brigade arrived in west area. Following is list of billets:— Dvl Headquarters VAULX. Mobile Veterinary Section CANDINVILLE K.D.Gs. GUERSHART T Battery, R.H.A. TOLLENT. 29th Lancers {FONTAINE L'ETALON (Headquarters) CHERRIENNE 36th Jacob's Horse GENNE-IVERGNY. BOUFFLERS (Headquarters).	A.S.D.C. Task

(73989) W4141—463. 400,000. 9/14. H.&J. Ltd. Forms/C. 2118/10.

Army Form C. 2118.

WAR DIARY
or
INTELLIGENCE SUMMARY.
(Erase heading not required.)

Instructions regarding War Diaries and Intelligence Summaries are contained in F. S. Regs., Part II. and the Staff Manual respectively. Title pages will be prepared in manuscript.

Hour, Date, Place	Summary of Events and Information	Remarks and references to Appendices
VAULX		
26/3/16.	Machine Gun Squadron CAUMONT.	
	Josephine Lancers { VILLEROY-SUR-AUTHIE VITZ-VILLEROY. PONCHEL. P^t. PONCHEL. DOEUX. LANNOY.	
27/3/16.	O.C. R.H.A. 10th Regimental Horse Transport Sergeant Nowid Floud reported his arrival. —	
28/3/16.	Went with field Transport to arrange supply of wood for the R^t. — Tried in AUXI-LE-CHATEAU and LATROYE, but no wood available. — Eventually made arrangements to cut wood in forest close to HAUTEVILLE. —	A.S.C.D. Rep^t.
29/3/16.	Fatigue Party of 2/9th Lancers went out to cut wood. — 6 Waggon loads brought in for Stoves. —	

Army Form C. 2118.

WAR DIARY
or
INTELLIGENCE SUMMARY.
(Erase heading not required.)

Instructions regarding War Diaries and Intelligence Summaries are contained in F.S. Regs., Part II and the Staff Manual respectively. Title pages will be prepared in manuscript.

Hour, Date, Place	Summary of Events and Information	Remarks and references to Appendices
VADIX		
27/3/16.	Before H. & truck proceeded on 7 days leave, otherwise orders in to G.D.S.O. to hand transport —	B.S.O.P. Left.

SERIAL NO. 244

Confidential

War Diary

of

Brigade Supply Officer, Lucknow Cavalry Brigade

FROM 1st April 1916 TO 30th April 1916.

Army Form C. 2118.

WAR DIARY
or
INTELLIGENCE SUMMARY. Lucknow Cavalry Brigade
(Erase heading not required.)

Instructions regarding War Diaries and Intelligence Summaries are contained in F.S. Regs., Part II and the Staff Manual respectively. Title pages will be prepared in manuscript.

Hour, Date, Place	Summary of Events and Information	Remarks and references to Appendices
VAUX 1/4/16 — 7/4/16	Routine duties — daily. Hay received at 14 lbs per animal from Reinforcements from 3rd Inst — 10 lbs from Railhead, 4 lbs from Divisional Reserve at AUXI-LE-CHATEAU — Captain A.F.R. Spode returned from 7 days leave, & resumed duties of B.R.S.O. (relieved Lieut GP²ᵈ) —	
8/4/16	Hay ration from Railhead reduced to 10 lbs per animal — No extra available in this area — Brigade issued preparations to move own forage 4 weeks training — list of billets below —	A.9.95 Sept.
YVRENCH 9/4/16	Brigade Headquarters YVRENCH. 29th Lancers YVRENCH and YVRENCHEUX 36th Jacob's Horse GAPENNES. Machine Gun Squadron GAPENNES. U. Battery R.H.A ARGENVILLERS. Jodhpur Lancers ARGENVILLERS. King's Dragoon Guards — NEUF MOULIN. —	

WAR DIARY or **INTELLIGENCE SUMMARY.** Mechanical Transport Brigade

Army Form C. 2118.

(Erase heading not required.)

Hour, Date, Place	Summary of Events and Information	Remarks and references to Appendices
9/4/15 continued YVRENCH	As supplies had not been divided up for those remaining behind in OLD PILLH, & the remainder of the G/13 in the west area, the lorries visited to the Old billets direct, in the morning, & to the new area in the afternoon. — Rendezvous at 2 p.m. at Four Roads N.E. of LE FESTEL on the AUXI-LE-CHATEAU - ST RIQUIER Road. — Went to ST RIQUIER with said Transport, to arrange for the supply of wood & water. — All potatoes had to be taken out from VAUX. — Flour very difficult to obtain. — Routine duties. —	O.E.G.O. top:
10/4/16 - 14/4/16 VAULX 15/4/16.	Brigade returned to Old billets. — Headquarters VAULX. — Routine duties. —	O.E.G.O. top
16/4/16 - 21/4/16. 22/4/16	Went to AUXI-LE-CHATEAU to interview Monsieur EDMOND VAQUETTE. (vide letter No. 550 1330 14-4-16 from O.C. M.T.C.) - Head Qrt	

Army Form C. 2118.

WAR DIARY
or
INTELLIGENCE SUMMARY.

(Erase heading not required.) Lucknow Cavalry Brigade

Instructions regarding War Diaries and Intelligence Summaries are contained in F.S. Regs., Part II. and the Staff Manual respectively. Title pages will be prepared in manuscript.

Hour, Date, Place	Summary of Events and Information	Remarks and references to Appendices
VAULX Continued — 22/4/16	he was not Touring to AUXI-LE-CHATEAU this week —	
23/4/16 – 25/4/16.	Routine duties. —	
26/4/16.	Went to FREVENT to interview Monsieur _____ with regard to supply of hay. — found that the following places only, in this area, are under him:— CAUMONT – VAULX – TOLLENT – FONTAINE – L'ETALON – GENNE IVENGNAY – PONCHEL.— He tells me very little hope of getting any oats, but promised a report within a week.— 2nd Lieut Thompson proceeded on leave.— Received report from 29th Lancers that they were experiencing difficulty in getting potatoes & that price had risen from F.11.50 per 100 K. to F 13/-/-	A.S.G.O. Taf? Q.S.G.O. Taf?
27/4/16	Sent to FONTAINE L'ETALON, with instructions, to arrange potatoes for 29th Lancers.—	

WAR DIARY
or
INTELLIGENCE SUMMARY.

(Erase heading not required.) Lucknow Infantry Brigade

Army Form C. 2118.

Hour, Date, Place	Summary of Events and Information	Remarks and references to Appendices
VAULX. 27/4/16 (cont:)	Was unable to interview the Mayor, but saw M. Bruggart & M. Doucher. The latter informed me that a private contractor, named M. Kabutte, had been round collecting potatoes, for which he was paying at much as F13/- per 100 K⁵ - M. Doucher declared F11/50 a fair price, & thought that about 5000 K⁵ should still be available. He gave me the names of divers farmers who, he thought, still had potatoes. I gave these names to the Gendarmerie of 29th Lancers. Based following amounts of wood to work, from LABROYE Forest:- 36th Jacob's Horse 2400 K⁵ Jodhpore Lancers. 2000 K⁵ Others units in Bde. 1440 K⁵	G.S.O.C. Inf.¹
28/4/16	Went to HESDIN, with interpreter, & interviewed M. RETS PAILLE. The following places in this area are under his control :- CAYMONT-CHERRIENNE -	G.S.O.C. Inf.¹

Army Form C. 2118.

WAR DIARY
or
INTELLIGENCE SUMMARY.

(Erase heading not required.) Frelinghien Cavalry Brigade

Instructions regarding War Diaries and Intelligence Summaries are contained in F.S. Regs., Part II. and the Staff Manual respectively. Title pages will be prepared in manuscript.

Hour, Date, Place	Summary of Events and Information	Remarks and references to Appendices
VAULX.		
28/4/16 (contd).	He informed me that he had also had difficulty with the Echelote, over getting particulars. — He came to CHERRIENNE with me, & arranged to let me have 25% of the amount of potatoes he was requisitioning in this place, for the French army. — Received instruction that the D.3. will be moving out to Training Area on 1st May. —	A.S.T.S. Pap.
29/4/16.	Went to Training Area & arranged for wood, in the following places:— POULONVILLERS — LE FESTEL — ONEUX. — Rate for wood: F. 2-50 per 100 K.3.— Practically no wood available at ONEUX, he arranged for the unit billeted there, to draw wood from LE FESTEL. — Lords only arrange one day's supply at ONEUX. —	A.S.T.S. Pap.
30/4/16.	Went to ST RIQUIER and MAISON ROLLAND to arrange wood. — Rate for wood: F. 3-0 per 100 K.3. —	A.S.T.S. Pap.

SERIAL NO. 244

Confidential

War Diary

of

Supply Officer, Lucknow Cavalry Brigade

FROM 1st May 1916 TO 31st May 1916.

Army Form C. 2118.

WAR DIARY
or
INTELLIGENCE SUMMARY.

(Erase heading not required.) *Unknown Cavalry Brigade*

Instructions regarding War Diaries and Intelligence Summaries are contained in F. S. Regs., Part II. and the Staff Manual respectively. Title pages will be prepared in manuscript.

Hour, Date, Place	Summary of Events and Information	Remarks and references to Appendices
ST RIQUIER. 1/5/16	Brigade marched to ST RIQUIER area for a week's training.— Billeting area as follows:— Brigade Headquarters ST RIQUIER Mobile Vet? Section K. D. G.s 16th Lancers / Jacob's Horse 2 Squadrons / Before Lancers Machine Gun Squadron — LE FESTEL. 2 Squadrons / Before Lancers — NEUVILLE. 2 9th Lancers — ONEUX — Arrangements made for potatoes & food to be had out from Railhead daily to training area, in lorries.— Ten detachments of units, left behind, following arrangements made:— Rations to be sent to be drawn daily from Railhead, on unimitated Transport (one Cart per unit was left behind for this purpose).—	A.C.B.O. Inf?

(73969) W4141—463. 400,000. 9/14. H.&J.Ltd. Forms/C. 2118/10.

Army Form C. 2118.

WAR DIARY
or
INTELLIGENCE SUMMARY.

(Erase heading not required.) Lucknow Cavalry Brigade.

Instructions regarding War Diaries and Intelligence Summaries are contained in F.S. Regs., Part II. and the Staff Manual respectively. Title pages will be prepared in manuscript.

Hour, Date, Place	Summary of Events and Information	Remarks and references to Appendices
1/5/16 (cont) ST. RIQUIER	All detachments able to arrange for potatoes & wood, except 4 D.G's, who drew potatoes & wood from Bde Headquarters. —	
2/5/16	Routine duties — Lieut Kingscote B.T.O. proceeded on leave. —	
3/5/16	Lieut F.I.F. FESTEL x 11 mired wood to 29th Lancers —	B.G.G.S. Top
4/5/16 – 5/5/16	Routine duties. —	
6/5/16	Received orders that the Brigade will move from present VAULX area on 10th that :- following places allotted to Luckow Bde :- REBREUVE – SERICOURT – SIBIVILLE – MONCHEAUX – CANETTEMONT — Lorries delivered rations for the whole Brigade, in the VAULX area. —	
VAULX 7/5/16	Lorries delivered rations for whole Brigade, in VAULX area — Brigade returned from Training Area to VAULX area. — 2 Squadrons Jodhpore Lancers detached to REBREUVE, to take over stores etc. — Went to REBREUVE & arranged for potatoes & wood for	B.G.G.S. Top

Army Form C. 2118.

WAR DIARY
or
INTELLIGENCE SUMMARY.

(Erase heading not required.) Lucknow Cavalry Brigade

Instructions regarding War Diaries and Intelligence Summaries are contained in F.S. Regs., Part II. and the Staff Manual respectively. Title pages will be prepared in manuscript.

Hour, Date, Place	Summary of Events and Information	Remarks and references to Appendices
VAULX 7/5/16 (contd)	above detachment.— Rations for consumption on 8th & 9th delivered to detachment on lorries." 2 Kent Transport returned from week's leave.	
8/5/16	Received list of Villages as follows, from Staff Captain :— Brigade Headquarters ⎫ U. Battery R.H.A. ⎬ REBREUVE.— Jodhpore Lancers ⎭ Machine Gun Squadron ⎫ HONVAL. Mobile Vet. Section ⎭ 29th Lancers CANETTEMONT 36th Jacob's Horse MONCHEAUX. K.D.G's. SERICOURT SIBIVILLE.— Information received from Staff Captain that 50 men 829th Lancers were being left behind at VACQUERIETTE to Various new area with F.R.O. & arranged for wood & potatoes.— Difficulty in getting wood at MONCHEAUX.	A.S.D.S. Capt. —
9/5/16		

(73989) W4141—463. 400,000. 9/14. H.&J.Ltd. Forms/C. 2118/10.

WAR DIARY
or
INTELLIGENCE SUMMARY

Army Form C. 2118.

(Erase heading not required.) Lucknow Cavalry Brigade

Instructions regarding War Diaries and Intelligence Summaries are contained in F.S. Regs., Part II. and the Staff Manual respectively. Title pages will be prepared in manuscript.

Hour, Date, Place	Summary of Events and Information	Remarks and references to Appendices
VAULX. 9/5/16 (cont)	Went round VAULX area to purchase potatoes to be carried to new area, under instructions from I.E.O. — Managed to get 2000 K⁰. —	O.S.P.C. Tpt.
REBREUVE 10/5/16.	Brigade arrived in new area. — Pickets as already given on 8th Inst: — 1000 K⁰. straw purchased in REBREUVE. —	
11/5/16.	All supplies drawn from Rebreuve on regimental transport, except Machine Gun Squadron, which had waggons from Auxiliary Horse Transport. — Went round all units in the B⁰⁰⁰ de. —	O.S.S.O. Tpt.
12/5/16.	Detachment of 30 men from 29th Lancers, returned to CANNETEMONT from VACQUERIETTES. — Iron rations brought to REBREUVE by lorries. —	

Army Form C. 2118.

WAR DIARY
or
INTELLIGENCE SUMMARY.

(Erase heading not required.) *Lucknow Cavalry Brigade*

Instructions regarding War Diaries and Intelligence Summaries are contained in F. S. Regs., Part II. and the Staff Manual respectively. Title pages will be prepared in manuscript.

Hour, Date, Place	Summary of Events and Information	Remarks and references to Appendices
REBREUVE 13/5/16.	Under orders G.O.C. H.S.C. the Bde has been lent to Divisional Headquarters as a temporary reserve. – Routine duties. –	Q.S.T.S.C. for
14/5/16 – 16/5/16.	Received instructions from S.S.O that the 1st Indian R.H.A. Bde (less G Battery) will march from REBREUVIETTE to 5th Divisional Area, halting at MINGOVAL on night of 18/19th May. – # V Battery echelons loaded on lorries, which will be sent to MINGOVAL on 18th inst. – Routine duties. –	

17/5/16 18/5/16	Received instructions from S.S.O. regarding arrangements made, if the Dismounted Brigade is ordered to hold itself in readiness. – Following Staff supplied from the Brigade:–
	 Brigade Transport Officer—Lieut Kingscote.
	      — Sergt Betteworth
	      — 1 N.C.O.
	      — Labour
	      — Weighmen
	 Informed that arrangements are being made to hand up from the Base, not more than one half American [reserve]
		Q.S.T.S.C. for

Army Form C. 2118.

WAR DIARY
or
INTELLIGENCE SUMMARY.

(Erase heading not required.) Lucknow Cavalry Brigade

Instructions regarding War Diaries and Intelligence Summaries are contained in F. S. Regs., Part II. and the Staff Manual respectively. Title pages will be prepared in manuscript.

Hour, Date, Place	Summary of Events and Information	Remarks and references to Appendices
REBREUVE 18/5/16 (Cont:)	Hang on Alfalfa.- Units have been informed accordingly.- Routine duties.-	
19/5/16 - 24/5/16	Inspection of this Brigade by Gen. C.-	
25/5/16	Received permission from S.S.O. for purchase of green forage for horses, when take received from Railhead is not above 10 lb per horse.- Total of purchases not to exceed the equivalent of 2 lb hay per horse.-	A.S.D.O. Tpt
26/5/16	Routine duties.-	
27/5/16		
28/5/16	Received orders from S.S.O. to discontinue purchase of potatoes for the present, as there is a three week's supply at the Dumps.- Routine duties.-	
29/5/16 =		
30/5/16	Arranged supply of green fodder for Bde. Headquarters Signal Troop & Mobile Vety Section, at RETS REUVE.- Shecta Futting.- Rate Fs 2/- per Kilo.	A.S.D.Q. Tpt
31/5/16	Arranged supply of green fodder for all units in G.H.Q. Area three kilometres above, North of HONVAL.- Rate Fs 1/-30 per kerge.-	

SERIAL NO. 244

Confidential
War Diary
of

Supply Officer, Lucknow Cavalry Brigade

FROM 1st June 1916 TO 30th June 1916.

Army Form C. 2118.

WAR DIARY
or
INTELLIGENCE SUMMARY.

(Erase heading not required.) Lucknow Cavalry Brigade.

Instructions regarding War Diaries and Intelligence Summaries are contained in F.S. Regs., Part II. and the Staff Manual respectively. Title pages will be prepared in manuscript.

Hour, Date, Place	Summary of Events and Information	Remarks and references to Appendices
RESERVE		
1/6/16.	Capt. Topham arranged for fatigue party of 40 men from 29th Lancers to cut fuel clover. Enough fuel for one day's supply. Fuel brought from O.C. A.S.C. Fatigue party of 60 men to cut clover.	O.C.S.O. Top.
2/6/16.	36th Jacob's Horse 40 men } one day's supply Machine Gun Squadron 10 " } cut.	
	Fatigue party of 70 men for cutting wood, discontinued from to-day, as 10 days' supply of wood is now in hand. Capt. Topham informed accordingly.	
3/6/16.	Fatigue party of 50 men to cut clover. Jodhpore Lancers 40 men } one day's supply Machine Gun Squadron 10 " } cut.	O.C.S.O. Top.
4/6/16.	Routine Duties.	
5/6/16.	Fatigue party for cutting clover, cancelled owing to bad weather. Inspection of Brigade Transport by O.C. A.S.C. 2.30 p.m. Received instructions from S.S.O. that 4 ozs potatoes per man may be issued to Indian Troops, when available, either from the Dumps or locally.	

WAR DIARY
or
INTELLIGENCE SUMMARY.

(Erase heading not required.) Lucknow Cavalry Brigade.

Army Form C. 2118.

Hour, Date, Place	Summary of Events and Information	Remarks and references to Appendices
REBREUVE 6/6/16.	Went to FREVENT with Requisitioning Officer, to try & procure fresh vegetables. Found it impossible to obtain at the rate laid down. Practically no fresh vegetables obtainable at present in this area. No green fodder cut, owing to bad weather.	
7/6/16.	Two days' supply of green fodder cut. Fatigue Parties as follows:— 9 A.M.–12 A.M. 40 men of 15th Lancers. (one day's supply) 2 P.M.–5 P.M. 40 men 36th Jacob's Horse } one day's supply 10 " Machine Gun Squadron	A.S.C. Tofts.
8/6/16.	One day's supply of green fodder cut. Fatigue Party as follows:— 40 men Jodhpur Lancers 10 men Machine Gun Squadron.	
9/6/16.	Received instructions from Major Captain Hoot Chown Tottery that Fatigue Parties for the Brigade are to cease. Each unit, in future, to do its own fatigue under Regimental arrangements.	A.S.C. Tofts.

Army Form C. 2118.

WAR DIARY
or
INTELLIGENCE SUMMARY.

(Erase heading not required.)

Lucknow Cavalry Brigade -

Hour, Date, Place	Summary of Events and Information	Remarks and references to Appendices
REBREUVE 9/6/16 (contd) - 10/6/16	B.R.O. visited units & arranged for fixtures - Following arrangements made for Green Fodder:- Headquarters } Machine Guns } F⁵ 1-20 per Verge, to last 1 week. Price Jodhpore Lancers F⁵ 1-20 " " " " 6 days * * When this amount is consumed, the Jodhpore Lancers will cut from the Brigade H.Q. grazing fields. - 29th Lancers F⁵ 1-0 per Verge, to last 8 days. - 36th Jacob's Horse F⁵ 1-0 " " " " " Auxiliary Horse Transport To } making their own K.D.G. } arrangements. -	A.S. & S.O. Infte.
11/6/16.	Routine Duties.- Received instructions from S.S.O. to draw the following from the Dump:- Potatoes 2000 lbs Onions 5000 "	C.E.G.G. Infte.

Army Form C. 2118.

WAR DIARY
or
INTELLIGENCE SUMMARY.

(Erase heading not required.) Lucknow Cavalry Brigade

Instructions regarding War Diaries and Intelligence Summaries are contained in F.S. Regs., Part II. and the Staff Manual respectively. Title pages will be prepared in manuscript.

Hour, Date, Place	Summary of Events and Information	Remarks and references to Appendices
REBRENE		
12/6/16.	Routine duties. —	
13/6/16.	Received R.s 5000 gomier from the Dump. —	
14/6/16.	Received R.s 1818 of Potatoes from the Dump. —	
15/6/16.	One Officer & 50 Ptd/Std O.R. from K. D. G.s (dismounted), left to-day for work in 17th Coys area. — This party will draw rations for consumption 17th & onwards, from 51st Division. — Fatigue party of 10 men from Supply Coy to put up wagons for the 200 O.R., will arrive, left to-day, from work in 7th Coys area. — This party has been rationed up to & for 17th inst.:—	A.E.G.S.C. Copy 5.
16/6/16.	Received preliminary instructions from I.S.O. That 300 men from 2nd Ind. Cavalry Regt. are moving from the Div:n to-morrow, as working party:— Rations for consumption on 19th, which are already with regiments, will be taken and on 2 f.S. waggons from	
17/6/16.	Regimented Transport. — Rations for consumption on 20th for the Working Party, will be loaded on lorries & moment Rations for those	A.E.G.S.C. Copy 5.

(73989) W4141—463. 400,000. 9/14. H.&J.Ltd. Forms/C. 2118/10.

Army Form C. 2118.

WAR DIARY
or
INTELLIGENCE SUMMARY.

(Erase heading not required.) Kitcheners Fighting Brigade

Instructions regarding War Diaries and Intelligence Summaries are contained in F.S. Regs., Part II. and the Staff Manual respectively. Title pages will be prepared in manuscript.

Hour, Date, Place.	Summary of Events and Information	Remarks and references to Appendices
RETREUVE 17/6/16 Cont.	remaining in Sibikli, will be loaded on G.S waggons as usual - tried to work for exact strengths going out Digging Party, & got the information to Ot. A.S.C & Ot. Supply Offr - Arranged for lorries to take out fuel & vegetables for Indemption at 20 k. -	A.S.C O Tept.
18/6/16.	Lieut G.S. Kingsell detailed as Transport Officer with above party - Working Party left the Brigade - Brighman Solamuddin detailed to accompany above party -	
19/6/16.	Information received from Offg Captain that 4½ Lancers & 36th Jacob's Horse are each lending up 4 Hotchkiss guns to-day, to join the Working Parties. - Received orders from S.S.O. to work strength of above detachments to Ot. Supply Offn & S.S.O. - Also requests for strengths & forwarded them, as ordered. -	A.S.G.G Tept.
20/6/16.	Received orders from Ot. A.S.C. to take over duties of Dt. Transport Officer during absence of Lieut Kingsell. -	
21/6/16.	Routine duties. -	

Army Form C. 2118.

WAR DIARY
or
INTELLIGENCE SUMMARY.

(Erase heading not required.) [Lucknow Cavalry Brigade.]

Instructions regarding War Diaries and Intelligence Summaries are contained in F.S. Regs., Part II. and the Staff Manual respectively. Title pages will be prepared in manuscript.

Hour, Date, Place	Summary of Events and Information	Remarks and references to Appendices
REBREUVE 22/6/16	Received orders from S.S.O. to communicate full strength of K.D.Gs to Supply Offr, for landing to - morrow. - Inspection of H.Q. Guards Transport by G.O.C. -	
23/6/16	Wrote to S.S.O. for instructions as to how the Regimental day's rations for Indians, is to be reached, in the event of orders being issued for it to be carried on the move. - Received information from Staff Captain that 1 Officer & 50 men of the K.D.Gs. are returning on 24th. - Routine duties. -	A.F.D.G. Toft.
24/6/16 - 25/6/16		
26/6/16	Went to S.T.P.O.L to arrange further Supply of wood for the D.22 Received instructions from S.S.O. that the two days' rations at present in hand, are to be handed over to units. - A brigade order 9462 Dated how rations in hand, have been handed over to Supply Officer Bris: Troops - A shortage of one day's biscuits came from Ghur, has been made up to me by Supply Officer Bris: Troops - Issued orders B.A.S.O, all available trs are being collected to pack the Ghur for above two Rations - the	A.F.D.G. Toft.

WAR DIARY
or
INTELLIGENCE SUMMARY

Army Form C. 2118.

Hour, Date, Place	Summary of Events and Information	Remarks and references to Appendices
PERREUSE 26/6/16 (cont.)		
27/6/16	Handed over charge of Brigade Transport to 2nd Lieut Knysett, who returned from duty with Working Party.	A.S.D.Pye
28/6/16	Received intimation from P.S.O. that one ounce Tea per squadron (fighting total), will be issued to supplement new Ration. Went to see Machine Gun Squadron, as O.C. reported Horses to be unable to carry the Gun Days' rations, having no wallets or packs, & only one G.S. wagon. — Totted up extra weight, for which transport is required, equals two tha- Would to O.C. ASC for instructions as to how this is to be carried.	
29/6/16	Received billets & ground area, from Staff Captain:— M.V.S. & 73rd Headquarters CROUCHES (left hand portion.) — K.D.G's CROUCHES (right —.) 2nd L. Lancers MILLY 36th Jacob's Horse BOUT des PRÉS. Machine Gun Squadron LA FOLIE FERME.	A.S.D.Pye

Army Form C. 2118.

WAR DIARY
or
INTELLIGENCE SUMMARY.

(Erase heading not required.) Lucknow Cavalry Brigade.

Instructions regarding War Diaries and Intelligence Summaries are contained in F.S. Regs., Part II and the Staff Manual respectively. Title pages will be prepared in manuscript.

Hour, Date, Place	Summary of Events and Information	Remarks and references to Appendices
REBREUVE. 29/6/16 (cont)	Units stand to march independently unto A+T Echelon. Starting point ARBRE. Lorries commenced delivering to-day, instead of yesterday. This procedure to continue until further orders. Only one day's rations in hand now. Received information from D Battery that they will arrive at REBREUVE at 4 am to-night. Have had their rations dumped ready for them. Following allocations ordered by S.S.O:- D Battery to be rationed by I.O. Div: Troops Amedier A.T. ↑₁ " " " " " " Supply Column " " " " " "	A.E.D.S.D. Foft.
GROUCHES. 30/6/16.	Brigade arrived in new area. Billets as already given. Arranged for supply of wood in forêt de LUCHEUX. Requisition but failed to dump at ESTREE WAMIN to draw five days bread & vegetables.	A.E.D.S.D. Foft.

SERIAL NO. 244.

Confidential

War Diary

of

Supply Officer, Lucknow Cavalry Brigade.

FROM 1st July 1916 TO 31st July 1916

Army Form C. 2118.

WAR DIARY
or
INTELLIGENCE SUMMARY.

Supply Officer
(Erase heading not required.) Inckmont Cavalry Brigade

Instructions regarding War Diaries and Intelligence Summaries are contained in F.S. Regs., Part II. and the Staff Manual respectively. Title pages will be prepared in manuscript.

Hour, Date, Place	Summary of Events and Information	Remarks and references to Appendices
BROUCHES. 1/7/16.	Routine duties.	
FROHEN-LE-GRAND	Brigade marched via HI VISEE — RANSART — BARLY — REMAISNIL — FROHEN-LE-GRAND. Starting Point: East Exit of RANSART at 6.30 p.m. Order of March: Brigade Headquarters, K.D.G's, Machine Gun Squadron, 36th Jacob's Horse, 29th Lancers, A Echelon in order of units. 73 Echelon in order of units. Mobile Veterinary Section. Billets as follows:—	A.S.D. Tot.
FROHEN-LE-GRAND	Dis Headquarters, K.D.G's. Mobile Veterinary Section.	
FROHEN-LE-PETIT	Machine Gun Squadron.	
VILLERS-L'HÔPITAL	29th Lancers, 36th Jacob's Horse. Got a loving from S.S.O. [illegible] from the [illegible] at ESTREE-WAMIN-[illegible]. The lorries had left the Brigade area before the order	C.S.D. Tot.

Army Form C. 2118.

WAR DIARY
or
INTELLIGENCE SUMMARY.
(Erase heading not required.) 1st Known Cavalry Brigade.

Instructions regarding War Diaries and Intelligence Summaries are contained in F.S. Regs., Part II. and the Staff Manual respectively. Title pages will be prepared in manuscript.

Hour, Date, Place	Summary of Events and Information	Remarks and references to Appendices
FROHEN-LE-GRAND 2/7/16 cont	to women, were received. — Telephoned to O.C. 1VC as to how to instruct men to the rear. — Divn. ordered to carry on work as previously arranged. — Issued instructions to units accordingly. — Information received about 5.20 p.m. that the lorries were returning, however field up to return. — Informed units accordingly. — Received a wire from S.S.O at 5.20 p.m. saying that the rendezvous for lorries would be at PISDUFTOUT, at 6 p.m. — left by L Return went to Supply Establishment to draw with the lorries. — Went to the rendezvous with 1st Transport O. — got a car as the rendezvous brought lorries to billeting area. — Issue of rations finished, & lorries went off by 9 p.m. —	A.S.O.S Top [?]
3/7/16	Rendezvous for lorries — VILLERS L'HÔPITAL at noon. Had lorry to Divnl at ESTREE WAMIN, to draw	A.S.O.S Top E.

Army Form C. 2118.

WAR DIARY
or
INTELLIGENCE SUMMARY.

(Erase heading not required.) Kitchener Cavalry Brigade

Instructions regarding War Diaries and Intelligence Summaries are contained in F. S. Regs., Part II and the Staff Manual respectively. Title pages will be prepared in manuscript.

Hour, Date, Place	Summary of Events and Information	Remarks and references to Appendices
FROHEN-LE-GRAND 3/7/16 cont	Five days supply of food in reserve. Received 5 the grain ration per horse, for to-morrow. 9 Hotchkiss machine Gun Gunners. This completes the Reserve Ration of oats per horse, for the whole D.T.	A.S.S.D. Toft.
	At VILLERS L'HOPITAL given an rendezvous for lorries to-morrow at noon. This was cancelled at 11.20 a.m. & AUXI LE CHATEAU given instead.	
4/7/16	Went to meet the lorries at AUXI LE CHATEAU, too hot found that the lorries had gone to VILLERS L'HOPITAL, where I went. Received ... from KD73 & 38th Jacob's Horse, regarding potatoes - Inspected potatoes myself & condemned them - gave orders to return by local purchase, pending orders from S.S.O. to return, a report has been sent. Attended a conference of Brigade supply officers at the office of our A.S.C.	A.S.S.D. Toft.

(73989) W4141—463. 400,000. 9/14. H.&J.Ltd. Forms/C. 2118/10.

Army Form C. 2118.

WAR DIARY
or
INTELLIGENCE SUMMARY.

(Erase heading not required.) Matthews Cavalry Brigade

Instructions regarding War Diaries and Intelligence Summaries are contained in F.S. Regs., Part II and the Staff Manual respectively. Title pages will be prepared in manuscript.

Hour, Date, Place	Summary of Events and Information	Remarks and references to Appendices
FROHEN-LE-GRAND 5/7/16.	Rendezvous for exercise - Day, 2.30 p.m., at entrance AUXI-LE-CHATEAU - ABBEVILLE Road. Drew two days supply of vegetables & bread from the dump at ESTREE-WAMIN. -	
6/7/16.	Rendezvous for exercise, 2.30 p.m. at entrance AUXI-LE-CHATEAU - WILLENCOURT Road. - Received 1470 lbs vegetables, 40 cwt road, & 10 cwt forage food from dump at ESTREE-WAMIN. - Informed by S.S.O. that Rendezvous will be PREVENT on 7th. -	C.S.57.51 Inf E
7/7/16.	Rendezvous for exercise, 2.30 p.m. at entrance AUXI-LE-CHATEAU - ABBEVILLE Road. - Informed by S.S.O that there is no necessity to attend Rendezvous in future, except in case of a move. -	
9/7/16.	Received 2240 lbs vegetables from the dump. - Weighmen Khinati returned from hospital. - Routine duties. -	C.S.57.51 Inf E
10/7/16.	Received 87 cwt road & 2897 lbs vegetables from Divisional Dump.	

Army Form C. 2118.

WAR DIARY
or
INTELLIGENCE SUMMARY.

(Erase heading not required.) Machine Gun Infantry Brigade

Instructions regarding War Diaries and Intelligence Summaries are contained in F. S. Regs., Part II, and the Staff Manual respectively. Title pages will be prepared in manuscript.

Hour, Date, Place.	Summary of Events and Information.	Remarks and references to Appendices.
FROHEN-LE-GRAND		
11/7/16.	Brigade put on 8 hours notice.	
12/7/16 – 13-7-16.	Routine duties.	
14/7/16.	Received information from Bde/ HQrs that the Brigade will move to-morrow – later received orders that move will take place on Sunday.	A. & Q. D. forts
15/7/16.	Received information from Staff Captain that move has been postponed.	
16/7/16.	Received following from the Dump at AUXI-LE-CHATEAU:– Vegetables 14.50 lbs. Bread 35 cwts.– Forage Total 12 cwts.–	
17/7/16.	Routine duties.–	
18/7/16.	Received the following from Divi Dump at AUXI-LE-CHATEAU :– Vegetables 1500 lbs. Bread 38 cwts. Forage Total 11 cwts."	A. & Q. D. forts

Army Form C. 2118.

WAR DIARY
or
INTELLIGENCE SUMMARY.

(Erase heading not required.) Lucknow Cavalry Brigade.

Hour, Date, Place.	Summary of Events and Information.	Remarks and references to Appendices.
FROHEM-LE-GRAND 18/7/16 Cont.	Received intimation from Staff Captain that the Brigade will move to-morrow. — Units ordered to Each End in two representations on the lorries returning empty to Railhead — Here to representations to accompany loaded lorries to warrants to the new area. —	A.P.G.G. Soft.
VILLERS-BRULIN 19/7/16.	Brigade moved to new area :- Billets as follows :- Dismounted men moved by train to TINCQUES :- Headquarters Mobile Vet: Section } VILLERS-BRULIN. 38th Field Amb. 1st K.D. Guards. } CAMBLIGNEUL 29th Lancers Machine Gun Squadron BETHENCOURT. I went to Divisional Rendezvous Box lorries at 9 A.M. at TINCQUETTE. — Lorries proceeded direct to appointed billets, as given above,	A.S.G.G. Soft.

Army Form C. 2118.

WAR DIARY
or
INTELLIGENCE SUMMARY.

(Erase heading not required.) [Lucknow Cavalry Brigade]

Instructions regarding War Diaries and Intelligence Summaries are contained in F. S. Regs., Part II, and the Staff Manual respectively. Title pages will be prepared in manuscript.

Hour, Date, Place.	Summary of Events and Information.	Remarks and references to Appendices.
VILLERS-BRULIN 19/7/18 (cont)	Where supplies were dumped in charge of the Force Representatives.	
20/7/18	Reconnoitring Officers made arrangements for Supply Issues. Received intimation from 5.50 that Jodhpore Lancers were withdrawn by Indian Cavalry Corps from Supply Railhead at Fressin and given to Supply Railhead at TINQUES. Received intimation from Staff Captain that 5th D.G. will furnish a Travel Party of 500 men, exclusive of the proper proportion of N.C.Os & British Officers. The Jodhpore Lancers will furnish 100 dismounted men for the above Party. The above parties to proceed under Brigade arrangements to mornings. Following, is list of Billets for above party:— Advanced Brigade Hd Quarters ECOIVRES— K.D. Guards – MONT ST ELOY – 29th Lancers } 36th Jacob's Horse } MAROEUIL Jodhpore Lancers }	A.G.G.T. Tpt. A.G.G.T. Tpt.

Army Form C. 2118.

WAR DIARY
or
INTELLIGENCE SUMMARY.

(Erase heading not required.) Lucknow Cavalry Brigade

Instructions regarding War Diaries and Intelligence Summaries are contained in F. S. Regs., Part II, and the Staff Manual respectively. Title pages will be prepared in manuscript.

Hour, Date, Place.	Summary of Events and Information.	Remarks and references to Appendices.
VILLERS-BRULIN 19/7/16 (cont.)	The advance parties to arrive at Villers by 4 p.m. — To take up unexpended portion of 3 days rations, & also rations for consumption on 21st. — Requested arrangements to be made for transporting above supplies, & daily, until further orders. —	A.E.T.S.O. Lieut.
20/7/16	Divisional Rendezvous TINCQUE at 9 A.M. — Went to Transit Camp & saw 2 vans Indians forcibly detained. Vegetables at boys for British & 2 boys for Indian Released on lorries for whole Bde. — Received 80 carts food from Divisional Dump at TINCQUE. —	
21/7/16	Divisional Rendezvous TINCQUE at 9 A.M. — Vegetables sent out by Supply to ou lorries. — Agent NANAK CHAND left this Brigade, being under orders to return to India. — Regtl. Havay, 1st 7 Lrs, reported his arrival for duty with this Bde. —	B.G.O. Lieut.

Army Form C. 2118.

WAR DIARY
or
INTELLIGENCE SUMMARY.

(Erase heading not required.) Luckrow Family Brigade

Hour, Date, Place.	Summary of Events and Information.	Remarks and references to Appendices.
VILLERS-BRULIN		
22/7/16.	Rendezvous TINCQUE at 10 am.	
23/7/16.	Ten Carts in to supply Column for fortnights rations. Received rations from Divisional Dump at TINQUES:- Drawn on Regimental Transport.	A.S.C. S.O Toft.
24/7/16.	Routine Duties:-	
25/7/16.	Received 2 days food from Divisional Dump. Ten returned from Famous Workshops.	
26/7/16.	Received orders from P.O to purchase Green Vegetables (except potatoes & onions) to make up the ration, until vegetables come up in sufficient quantities from Railhead S:- Routine duties.	A.S.C. Toft.
27/7/16. 28/7/16.	Ten returned to O.C. A.S.C. Reinforcements (50 men his kits) arrived for 29th Lancers & 36th Jacob's Horse, from MARSEILLES.- No Iron Rations with men 29th Lancers.	
29/7/16.	Received information from Staff Captain that Exchange for East	

Army Form C. 2118.

WAR DIARY
or
INTELLIGENCE SUMMARY.

(Erase heading not required.) Lucknow Cavalry Brigade

Instructions regarding War Diaries and Intelligence Summaries are contained in F. S. Regs., Part II, and the Staff Manual respectively. Title pages will be prepared in manuscript.

Hour, Date, Place.	Summary of Events and Information.	Remarks and references to Appendices.
VILLERS-BRULIN. 29/7/16 (cont.)	for MARSEILLES probably leave Reichlands on 1st August - five days copies returned to this latter by this party. - Three rations have been indented for. - Double teams of Rations at 10.30 A.M. & 4.30 P.M.	B.E.F. G. Jaft
30/7/16.	Received intimation from Staff Captain that Exchange party of Indians for MARSEILLES is to be at Railhead by 4.15 pm on 1st. - The party will be in charge of Lieut: Chubb, 38th Jacob's Horse. - Rations for consumption on 1st mixed to-day of 4 prs. & 4 Indian meat. Brigade HQ. Quarters moved from VILLERS-BRULIN to CHELLERS. - A.D.S.(?) ordered to send a party of 20 men for work at ANZIN on 1st inst. - Asked O.C. Supply Col. to have rations for the above party transferred to the Field Canteen, to whom they will be attached. - No issue of rations to-day except the rations for the MARSEILLES party & Indian meat. -	B.E.F. G. Jaft
CHELLERS 31/7/16.		

SERIAL NO. 244.

Confidential

War Diary

of

Supply Officer, Lucknow Cavalry Brigade.

FROM 1st August 1916 TO 31st August 1916.

Army Form C. 2118.

WAR DIARY

INTELLIGENCE SUMMARY. Supply Officer

(Erase heading not required.) Lucknow Cavalry Brigade.

Instructions regarding War Diaries and Intelligence Summaries are contained in F. S. Regs., Part II, and the Staff Manual respectively. Title pages will be prepared in manuscript.

Hour, Date, Place.	Summary of Events and Information.	Remarks and references to Appendices.
CHELLERS 1/8/16	K.D. Guards moved from CAMBLIGNEUL to MONCHY-BRETON	
2/8/16	29th Lancers " " " to CHELLERS. —	
	S.S.O. & O.C. Supply Coy informs of above moves. — Routine duties. —	A.S.C. O. Reft.
3/8/16	Arranged Supply of 9 mens horses for 30th Jaco Squadron & 29th Lancers. Routine duties. —	
4/8/16 – 5/8/16	Received information from 30th Major that the 30th will move into new area on 9th. — Supply Officer Div. Troops informs that the Lucknow Cavalry Bde. Ambulance will be attached to this 30th from 10th inst. Which him for 'things. — Asked I.S.O. up to what date vehicles I am to retain the Telephone Lorries. —	
6/8/16	Received intimation from Staff Captain that arrangements have been made by the D.I.S. for the District & Horse Watering of this 30th to be delivered at SAVETY from 9th inst. inclusive. —	G.S.C.O. Reft.

WAR DIARY

Army Form C. 2118.

Instructions regarding War Diaries and Intelligence Summaries are contained in F. S. Regs., Part II, and the Staff Manual respectively. Title pages will be prepared in manuscript.

(Erase heading not required.) Lucknow Cavalry Brigade.

Hour, Date, Place.	Summary of Events and Information	Remarks and references to Appendices.
CHELLERS. 7/8/16.	Dismounted men of K.D.G's, 34th Lancers & 38th J. Horse will move by lorry to moved to next area.— The following will leave the Bde. to-morrow on detachment:— British Indian Animals S.D.C. N/2 G." 70 — 25 K.D.G's 185 — 203 38th J. Horse 3 147 157 M.G. Squadron 33 — u.u.? The above information has been had to the S.S.O. who 1st I.C.D. Pujabis — S.S.O. asked who will arrange rations for this body.— Later I received orders from O.C. K.S.C. that I was to arrange rations for above body.— Double issue of Rations for the whole Brigade for To-morrow—Sumption on 8th & 9th, except Indian meat for 9th, which will be issued to-morrow—	a.s.g.o. lt.
8/8/16	The issue of Indian meat for consumption on 9th was not made to-day — Consequently, the B.D. is one day's Indian meat short —	a.s.g. lt.

Army Form C. 2118.

WAR DIARY

~~INTELLIGENCE SUMMARY.~~

(Erase heading not required.) Lucknow Cavalry Brigade.

Instructions regarding War Diaries and Intelligence Summaries are contained in F. S. Regs., Part II, and the Staff Manual respectively. Title pages will be prepared in manuscript.

Hour, Date, Place.	Summary of Events and Information	Remarks and references to Appendices.
CHELLERS 8/8/16 cont.	The Detached Party arrived in the St Pol area – Billets as follows:– Brigade Headquarters – ST. POL and BRYAS K.D. Guards. – HERNICOURT. 36th Jacob's Horse – GAUCHIN. Machine Gun Squadron – HERNICOURT. I went over to St. Pol with Staff Regt Newman, who I left in charge temporarily. – Arranged for Office etc.– The Divn units viz 9 K.D Guards, 29th Lancers & 36th Jacobs Horse less present billets, in lorries, at 12 o'clock, for the new area. – Billets as follows:– K.D. Guards – HUMBERCAMP. – 29th Lancers – WARLINCOURT. – 36th Jacob's Horse – GAUDIEMPRE. – Rations for the whole Brigade, less St Pol PARTY, delivd in new area this afternoon for consumption on 10th. The lorries with the rations accompanied	A.S. 676 Sept. A.S. 676 Sept.

Army Form C. 2118.

Instructions regarding War Diaries and Intelligence
Summaries are contained in F. S. Regs., Part II.
and the Staff Manual respectively. Title pages
will be prepared in manuscript.

WAR DIARY
INTELLIGENCE SUMMARY
(Erase heading not required.) Lucknow Cavalry Brigade.

Hour, Date, Place	Summary of Events and Information	Remarks and references to Appendices
CHELERS 3/10/18 cont.	the dismounted men, who took over the rations, on arrival at the new billets. — Parties were sent on by B'n. Hd. Qrs and Lucknow Fd. Amb. to take over their rations. — In the afternoon I went to the PMS and with Field Trans- Ford & interviewed the Senior Supply Officer of the 46th. 157th Division at BAVINCOURT and WARLINCOURT — The following units are attached to 46th Div:— Brigade Hd. Qrs. R.D. Guards Machine Gun Squadron (less 2 section) The following units are attached to 58th Div:— 29th + 1 sec. M.G. Squadron Lancers 36th J. Horse " " Machine Gun Squadron (less 1 section). Lucknow Fd. Ambulance " " "	A.E.R.B. Capt. All rationed by the 73.S.S.0. 139th B/de. as far as Rations are concerned. 1395 B/de. Billets & Horses are concerned. by S.O. No 1 Sup 58th Div Train — A.G.B. Inf.

Army Form C. 2118.

WAR DIARY
INTELLIGENCE SUMMARY
(Erase heading not required.) Lucknow (Cavalry Brigade).

Instructions regarding War Diaries and Intelligence Summaries are contained in F.S. Regs., Part II. and the Staff Manual respectively. Title pages will be prepared in manuscript.

Hour, Date, Place	Summary of Events and Information	Remarks and references to Appendices
CHELLERS. 8/8/16 Cont	The following are the arrangements of 4th Div:—	
	Load in 2 groups, at the Station: - Group 1. B¹ & M² Guards	
	" 2. { K.D. Guards { M.G. Squadron	G.S.T.B. Tpts.
	Above are loaded at 3 a.m. & moved direct to the billets of the above groups at 9 a.m.—	
	B.S.S's to be detrained. Direct to Supply Officer 139 B.S.S. 1st. by units at time of moving in advance.— The B.S.S's to be for 4 days in advance.—	
	Units in this Div: are rationed up to 2 days ahead.—	
	Arrangements 9.55th Div: are as follows:—	
	Rations are drawn by B.S's in bulk at 1. a.m. & dumped at 11 a.m. at Goods Supply Officer's dump.— Units draw rations in their own transport at 7 A.M.— B.S.S's for 4 days in advance to be handed to it's own Supply Officer in	G.S.T.B. Tpts
	bulk at time of moving.— Rations Units in this Div: are rationed up to 1 day ahead.—	

Army Form C. 2118.

WAR DIARY
INTELLIGENCE SUMMARY.
(Erase heading not required.)

Instructions regarding War Diaries and Intelligence Summaries are contained in F.S. Regs., Part II. and the Staff Manual respectively. Title pages will be prepared in manuscript.

Hour, Date, Place	Summary of Events and Information	Remarks and references to Appendices
CHELLERS - 8/8/16 (cont)	Reitland for both Divisions in SAPLIN. The S.S.O 19 I.C.D. has informed S.S.O's 9.45.15 x 58.D. Div re. booking of supply train. First delivery of rations by 46th Div: on 9th, & 58th Div on 10th for consumption on 11th. I left Lieut. Trawford at PAS, and returned to CHELLERS. Indian rations for the whole (B.P. Fontaine to be) drawn from TINQUES & are sent daily by lorries direct to units.	A.S.A.R. Foot
PAS 9/8/16	Brigade moved (less S.T POL party & dismounted men) moved into PAS area. I went to ST POL and to writers of rations at 10.30 by lorries from TINQUES.	A.S.A.R. Foot

Army Form C. 2118.

WAR DIARY
INTELLIGENCE SUMMARY

(Erase heading not required.) Lucknow Cavalry Brigade.

Instructions regarding War Diaries and Intelligence Summaries are contained in F.S. Regs., Part II. and the Staff Manual respectively. Title pages will be prepared in manuscript.

Hour, Date, Place	Summary of Events and Information	Remarks and references to Appendices
PAS 9/8/16 cont.	Bde. Major informed me that S.E. Force detachment, (less one troop R.H.G., Hd. G.S. and 2 sections M.G. Squadron) will march to PAS over to-morrow to rejoin Bde. - I informed P.S.O. 1st & 2nd Div. H.Q.C. R.H.D. Fol. Supply about change & gave revised figures to supply for S.E. Foz Party. Arranged for the rations balance of rations to be drawn - period from 1st Foz party & sent to PAS area for consumption on 11th. - I informed S.S.O's 48th & 56th Div. re regarding change in through of British & animals for consumption on 12th. - I remained at PAS. -	G.S.O. Fol. G.O.C. Fol.
10/8/16.	Routine duties. -	

Army Form C. 2118.

WAR DIARY
INTELLIGENCE SUMMARY.
(Erase heading not required.) Lucknow Cavalry Brigade

Instructions regarding War Diaries and Intelligence Summaries are contained in F.S. Regs., Part II. and the Staff Manual respectively. Title pages will be prepared in manuscript.

Hour, Date, Place	Summary of Events and Information	Remarks and references to Appendices
P.A.S. 11/8/16	Received information from H/qs [of] Division that the whole of the 37 POL detachment begins this B'de to-morrow. — Informed details for 8th Lancers & arranged for rations, etc. — Supervision 13th to be delivered in PAS area. — Informed R.S.O's of 46 & 38th Div: of increase in British & Horse rations for Lucknow 14th. —	A.E.L.B. hqts.
12/8/16	Arranged with Supply offices 139th B'de, 34 & 46th Div. for the supply of Green Fodder to Headquarters. —	
13/8/16		A.E.L.B. hqts.
14.5.16	Proceeded on leave & handed over duties to Lt. H. Crawford. Requisitioning Officer.	

WAR DIARY

INTELLIGENCE SUMMARY

(Erase heading not required.)

Army Form C. 2118.

Hour, Date, Place	Summary of Events and Information	Remarks and references to Appendices
Pos 15 U.	Visited S.S.O. Steenbecque regarding rations for units & ranks & animals to take unit to have two days in advance, also S.O.S. Steenbecque regarding issue of green fodder to unit when there.	Steenbecque
16 U.	As no vegetables for Indians were received to-day from railhead, they had to be purchased already (Turnips at 40/- per cwt.) Lancer unit S.O. had arrangements for green fodder for 29th Lancer unit S.O. kept dump of 2 days. Unit cutting its own requirements	Steenbecque
17 U.	Routine duties	
18 U.	Routine duties	

WAR DIARY or INTELLIGENCE SUMMARY

Army Form C. 2118.

Hour, Date, Place	Summary of Events and Information	Remarks and references to Appendices
PA 81 19.5.16	Rct S.O. advanced party 17th Div who are taking over from the 58th in neighbourhood of [Acheux?]. Met 29th Lancers & 36th Jacob's Horse & I.C. Field Amb. drew their rations from No 2 Div. dumps. 17th Div. D.A.D.T. approved the dumps as before. Rations from IZ same as usual.	St. Amand Lt.
20.5.16	36th Jacob's Horse & 29th Lancers received rations As Champ Veel to COULLEMONT & WARLUZEL arranged with S.S.O. & Column officer 17th Div. who supplied lorries to take the days ration for men on 21st but as was usual when St. Amand Lt. an advance party of the Regiment took the rea[tions].	St. Amand Lt.

Army Form C. 2118.

WAR DIARY
INTELLIGENCE SUMMARY
(Erase heading not required.) Lucknow Cavalry Brigade.

Instructions regarding War Diaries and Intelligence Summaries are contained in F. S. Regs., Part II. and the Staff Manual respectively. Title Pages will be prepared in manuscript.

Place	Date	Hour	Summary of Events and Information	Remarks and references to Appendices
PAS.	21.5.16		The 29th Lancers & 36th J.H. being in the area of now seen taken over by this Div. Jr rations. Arrangements arranged the 24th Lel. An other days ration was drawn today Jr. Brit. ranks & animals. The Brigade has now (with the reception of the L.C. Field Amb) two days ration in hand as desired by the S.S.O. 1st Ind. C.D. The DC Supply Col. 46th Div. is taking over from tomorrow after the hour of rations the lorries lent to the 51st Div. & handed over to 17th Div. in entirety.	Strength J. Lt.
	22.5.16		Routine duties. lorries taken over by 46th Div.	
	23.5.16		Routine duties. I modified over to Capt Byrd to be return Jr. leave.	Strength J. Lt.

Army Form C. 2118.

WAR DIARY
INTELLIGENCE SUMMARY

(Erase heading not required.) Lucknow Cavalry Brigade.

Place	Date	Hour	Summary of Events and Information	Remarks and references to Appendices
PAS	24/8/16		Routine duties. —	
	25/8/16		Received intimation from Staff Captain that the Lucknow Fd: Ambulance will move to-day from ST AMAND to LUCHEUX. — I arranged with the 17th Div: to return teams up to & for 27th Inst:, & the 46th Div: will return them from 28th onwards — Informed A.S.O. 1st Ind: Cav: Div: transport, plus two m.g. h.g. of the above move. —	A.B.S.P. 1st Ind...
	26/8/16 – 31/8/16.		Routine duties. —	

A. E. B. Ryles Copy: S.T.C.
B.S.O. Lucknow Cavalry Bde:
I.E.F.

SERIAL No. 244

Confidential
War Diary
of

Supply Officer, Lucknow Cavalry Brigade

FROM 1st September 1916 TO 30th September 1916

WAR DIARY or INTELLIGENCE SUMMARY

(Erase heading not required.) Lucknow Cavalry Brigade.

Army Form C. 2118.

Place	Date	Hour	Summary of Events and Information	Remarks and references to Appendices
PAS	1/9/16		Received intimation from Staff Captain that the Bde will move from present billets, on the 3rd, to the area bound FROHEM-LE-GRAND. - I arranged with the S.S.O. 46th Div that the lorries loading for Embarkation on 3rd 4th will deliver in new area on 3rd. - Rendezvous OCCOCHES at 11 a.m.- Arranged with 1st Inf. Bde for 1st Flag to lead the Russian motor lorries to above rendezvous at same time. In Emergence of above, there will be no issue of rations on 2nd. - The Bde will move to the ST RIQVIER training area on 4th. - I arranged with SSO 48th Div that rations drawn for Embarkation on 5th, will be dumped at SAULTY 1st. - When the lorries have issued on 3rd, they will at once proceed to SAULTY & pick up rations for Embarkation 5th, & park for the night at WARLUZEL. - They will proceed, under Lieut Shuttleworth, on the 4th to the ST RIQVIER area, & train & rendezvous will be notified later. -	G.S.A.B.
	2/9/16		No news of rations in Emergence of above. - Capt: C. John Knight, S.A.T Corps reported his arrival, to act as B.T.O during the absence of Lieut Knightall A.S.C, & assist with superintending duties until the return of Lieut Tempson. -	
OCCOCHES	3/9/16		Brigade marched from PAS to new area. - Route as follows:- LUCHEUX - BOUQUEMAISON - NEUVILLETTE. - Billets as follows :-	

Army Form C. 2118.

WAR DIARY
INTELLIGENCE SUMMARY.
Lucknow Cavalry Brigade

(Erase heading not required.)

Instructions regarding War Diaries and Intelligence Summaries are contained in F. S. Regs., Part II. and the Staff Manual respectively. Title Pages will be prepared in manuscript.

Place	Date	Hour	Summary of Events and Information	Remarks and references to Appendices
OCCOCHES	3/9/16	—	OCCOCHES { Bde Headquarters Mach. Vet. Section Machine Gun Squadron MEZEROLLES — K.D. Guards OUTREBOIS — 29th Lancers REMAISNIL — 36th Jacob's Horse BONNIERES — Lucknow (inc. F.s Ambulance) Rendezvous at 11 A.M. at OCCOCHES on main DOULLENS-AUXI road. The Indian rations were distributed by motor lorries before they moved off from Rendezvous. After embussing the lorries returned to SAVEUSE.	a.g. A.B.
BRAILLY	4/9/16	—	Brigade marched to new area by following route:- FROHEN-LE-GRAND - BEALCOURT-MAIZICOURT - HEIRMONT-YVRENCH- Billets as follows:- BRAILLY { Bde Headquarters Mob. Vet. Section Machine Gun Squadron CANCHY — K.D. Guards DONVAST — 29th Lancers GAPENNES — 36th Jacob's Horse ARGENVILLERS - Lucknow Four Ft Ambulance	a.s. A.B.

Army Form C. 2118.

WAR DIARY
INTELLIGENCE SUMMARY

(Erase heading not required.) Lucknow Cavalry Brigade

Place	Date	Hour	Summary of Events and Information	Remarks and references to Appendices
BRAILLY	4/9/16	—	Rendezvous Cross Roads in BRAILLY at 4 p.m. — The Indian rations were distributed by units, at the Rendezvous, before the lorries left. The empty lorries rejoined the 1st Indian Cav: Supply Col: at ST RIQUIER, the war railhead. — The Dismounted men of the Bde. marched to BUIRE-AU-BOIS. — Their rations are being sent out direct by the Retns: Sec: 1st Ind. Div. —	G.S.B.
BRAILLY	5/9/16	—	No Rendezvous — Lorries delivered direct to units at 2.30 P.M. —	
"	6/9/16	—	No Rendezvous — Lorries delivered direct to units at 10 A.M. — Unit Transports returned from leave. Draw one day's supply of food at 1.64 per man for the whole Bde, from the church at ST RIQUIER — Units drew the food from Hd Quarters, also vegetables at 2 ozs. per man	
BRAILLY	7/9/16	—	Handed over duties of A.S.O. to Capt: St: John Wright S.T.C.	
BRAILLY	8/9/16 9/16.10	—	Proceeded to England to report to India Office. Ordinary routine duties.	
FROHEN LE G.D. HEM QUERRIEUX ALBERT	11th 12th 13th 15th		Brigade moved to FROHEN LE GRAND AREA. Brigade " " HEM area. Brigade " " QUERRIEUX area. Brigade " " position between DERNANCOURT & MORLANCOURT 1m½ S. of ALBERT and remained here until 25th	O.W. R. O.W.
MONTAUBAN	26th		Brigade moved to MONTAUBAN (Head Qrs) units including "U" Battery R.H.A. and Field Ambulance in FRICOURT & MAMETZ	O.W.

Army Form C. 2118.

WAR DIARY
or
INTELLIGENCE SUMMARY
(Erase heading not required.)

Instructions regarding War Diaries and Intelligence Summaries are contained in F. S. Regs., Part II. and the Staff Manual respectively. Title Pages will be prepared in manuscript.

Place	Date Sept	Hour	Summary of Events and Information	Remarks and references to Appendices
BUSSY-LES-DAURS	27th	—	Brigade routine duties.	Qee
HANGEST SUR SOMME	28th		Brigade routine duties.	
Bois de l'Abbaye	29th		Brigade routine duties.	
CRECY en PONTHIEU	30th	1	Brigade routine duties.	

Auignacot
B.M.
Lucknow Cav. Bde.

30/9/16.

WO 95/11757

B.E.F.

1 Ind. Cav. Div.

Lucknow Bde.

Bde Transport Officer

1914 Nov — 1915 July

1916 July — 1916 Sept

267

WAR DIARY

of

Lucknow Bgde Transport Officer

From 16-11-14 To 25-12-14

Army Form C. 2118.

WAR DIARY
or
INTELLIGENCE SUMMARY.
(Erase heading not required.)

B or Transport.

Instructions regarding War Diaries and Intelligence Summaries are contained in F. S. Regs., Part II, and the Staff Manual respectively. Title pages will be prepared in manuscript.

Hour, Date, Place.	Summary of Events and Information.	Remarks and references to Appendices.
ORLEANS Nov 16/14	The transport was detrained by O.C. Horse Transport BERCOTTES Camp to the Lucknow Bde on arrival at ORLEANS.	
ORLEANS Dec 13 8th		
14th Dec 6.30 am LILLERS	Orders received to arrange to be ready to move at 1 hours notice. 1st & 2nd Transport were posted, with Carts fitted and the Brigade start to	
15th hour LILLERS 20 hour LILLERS	The Bde still ready to move at short notice Bde moved to area to an area MORRENT FONTES-ST KWAIRE-Rumilly	
25 Dec 2 Meuchin	Bde moved to area FIC-F.S.-PREDEFIN-LISBURG-MEUCHIN. Headquarters Transport was billeted at MEUCHIN. The Regtal Transport with their Regiments	

WAR DIARY

of

Brigade Transport, Lucknow Cavalry Brigade.

From 1-1-15   To 31-1-15.

Army Form C. 2118.

WAR DIARY
or
INTELLIGENCE SUMMARY. (Erase heading not required.)

Bde Transport

Hour, Date, Place.	Summary of Events and Information.	Remarks and references to Appendices
1st January 1915. HENCHIN	In billets Steenwerck area. Capt. T.W. [?] Bde Transport Officer.	
4th January HENCHIN	Received orders that Bde was to do 48 hours in trenches from evening 4th to evening 9th relieving SEAFORTH Bde Transport consisting of 9th & AT Carts and 1 water cart from each regiment between (Total 20 A.T Carts and 1 pony (signalling) from Headquarters to leave Cross Roads at SAINS for BETHUNE (Hqrs) to leave Cross Roads and to start the night of 8.9th at MARLES. 2 AT Carts from the R/S containing entrenchment tools and Pioneer + Signalling equipment. The Men & went empty this in order to take prisoners from BETHUNE Transport 20 AT Carts 1 Pony Tonga left SAINS Cross Roads at 11 am arrived MARLES at 2 p.m. Carts were parked along side road in MARLES and the animals in a field.	
8th January HENCHIN		
9th January MARLES.	Left MARLES 8.30 am arrived BETHUNE 11 am parked in the MARCHE aux Chevaux and commenced loading empty Carts with rations. The Brigade arrived BETHUNE at 4 pm detrained and marched to FESTUBERT	

WAR DIARY
or
INTELLIGENCE SUMMARY.

(Erase heading not required.)

Army Form C. 2118.

Instructions regarding War Diaries and Intelligence Summaries are contained in F. S. Regs., Part II, and the Staff Manual respectively. Title pages will be prepared in manuscript.

Hour, Date, Place.	Summary of Events and Information.	Remarks and references to Appendices.
9 Jan (continued) FESTUBERT	The transport moved on behind their Regiments into line of motorcars which marched rear of Bttn. The Motorcars were left parked at GORE. In Relief of STAFFORDS R. commenced at 7.2pm. The carts going into their Regiments to their headquarters and returned empty to Rue de Bethune — They were collected here at 3 am. ½ hr delay was owing to their being only one practicable road — the transport proceeded of track to BETHUNE at 3 am the transport proceeded of track to BETHUNE passing the staff of the Bde in relieving on the way, passing BETHUNE 6 am	
10 Jan FESTUBERT	Parked Transport in lee MERCIPE aux Chevaux 30 wagons were loaded with supplies at 11 am and started for FESTUBERT at 4 pm going to their Regtl headquarters after dark and were unloaded there. Carts again at BETHUNE Rue de BETHUNE at 11 pm and marched to GORE where they were parked for the night with the remaining carts which had been previously brought there from BETHUNE	
Jan; FESTUBERT	All the carts were sent to Regiments at 10 o'clock when they were loaded and marched back their Regiments to BETHUNE they were billetted and parked at Both MARCHE aux Chevaux up to 1 am.	

Army Form C. 2118.

WAR DIARY
or
INTELLIGENCE SUMMARY.
(Erase heading not required.)

Hour, Date, Place.	Summary of Events and Information.	Remarks and references to Appendices.
H.Q.ast BETHUNE 12 Jan.	Left BETHUNE at 8.30am arrived HEUCHIN at 4 pm. Carts were sent off to their regiments — there were no casualties and his men slept their carts very well considering his very bad state of the roads to YESTRUBER and they could only get to their regimental headquarters when it was pitch dark. The weather throughout was wet and the roads bad and extremely muddy.	
28 Jan HEUCHIN	The Indian Cavalry Corps was inspected by the Commander in Chief.	
29 Jan HEUCHIN	At 11 pm. Orders received for the Brigade to hold itself in readiness to move at 1 hour notice.	
30 Jan HEUCHIN	Brigade in a state of readiness.	
31 Jan HEUCHIN	Brigade in state of readiness.	

Whitehead Capt
R.T.O.
8 (Lucknow) Cav Bde

WAR DIARY

Brigade Transport Officer, Lucknow Cavalry Brigade.

From 1st February 1915 to 28th February 1915

Army Form C. 2118.

Lucknow Cav Bde
TRANSPORT

WAR DIARY
or
INTELLIGENCE SUMMARY.

(Erase heading not required.)

Instructions regarding War Diaries and Intelligence Summaries are contained in F. S. Regs., Part II, and the Staff Manual respectively. Title pages will be prepared in manuscript.

Hour, Date, Place.	Summary of Events and Information.	Remarks and references to Appendices.
Feb 1 – Feb 28 HEUCHIN	In billets HEUCHIN area.	

J Whitehead Capt
Brigade Transport Officer
Lucknow Cavalry Brigade

WAR DIARY

OF

Brigade Transport Officer, Lucknow Cavalry Brigade.

From 22nd April 1915 To 30th April 1915

Army Form C. 2118.

WAR DIARY
or
INTELLIGENCE SUMMARY.
(Erase heading not required.)

Instructions regarding War Diaries and Intelligence
Summaries are contained in F.S. Regs., Part II
and the Staff Manual respectively. Title pages
will be prepared in manuscript.

Hour, Date, Place	Summary of Events and Information	Remarks and references to Appendices
April 22nd/915 ESTRÉE BLANCHE	Took over duties of Brigade Transport Officer Lucknow Cavalry Brigade from Lieut. Sullivan, A.S.C.	
23rd	Routine duties in billets.	
24th - 17.30	Orders received for Brigade to move to neighbourhood of ST MARIE CAPPEL. Transport left turn churt of ESTRÉE BLANCHE 20.5. arriving in new billets at 6 am 25th inst. My casualties were 2 wagon's which had to be temporarily left. These recovered next day.	
25 - 27th ST MARIE CAPPEL	Routine duties in billets under 1 hours notice to move	
28th 14.00	Brigade marched to neighbourhood of WATOU. A echelon accompanied brigade under Lieut. BRADLEY. 29th San car. Remained with B echelon which was parked in ST MARIE CAPPEL under orders of O.C. A.S.C. 1st Cav. Division	
29th 15.25 ST MARIE CAPPEL	Orders received for B. Echelon transport to march to WATOU. Transport was ready to move 15.55. + marched	

(73989) W4141—463. 400,000. 9/14. H.&J.Ltd. Forms/C. 2118/10.

WAR DIARY
or
INTELLIGENCE SUMMARY.
(Erase heading not required.)

Army Form C. 2118.

Instructions regarding War Diaries and Intelligence Summaries are contained in F.S. Regs., Part II. and the Staff Manual respectively. Title pages will be prepared in manuscript.

Hour, Date, Place	Summary of Events and Information	Remarks and references to Appendices
ST JAN-TER-BIEZEN April 30-15	WM Remainder of Squadron & B Echelon to WATOU at 16.25 arriving 20.00 after marching over bricks in highway hard on casualties Ordinary routine duties	

A. Hurlof
O.C. Royal Drumfries Officers
W. Kent Cavalry Brigade

WAR DIARY

Transport (Lucknow Cavalry Brigade.) Head Quarters

From 1st May to 31st May 1915

Army Form C. 2118.

Instructions regarding War Diaries and Intelligence Summaries are contained in F.S. Regs., Part II. and the Staff Manual respectively. Title pages will be prepared in manuscript.

WAR DIARY
or
INTELLIGENCE SUMMARY.
(Erase heading not required.)

Hour, Date, Place	Summary of Events and Information	Remarks and references to Appendices
May 17th 1915 ST JAN-TER-BIEZEN	Routine in billets	
Aug 2nd 3.0 A.M. ST MARIE CAPPEL	Brigade marched to ST MARIE CAPPEL arriving 2 pm. Nolomette en route	
5th 2 aus.	Routine in billets	
MAMETZ G.S.R. 12 R. 14th	Brigade marched to MAMETZ. Battalion formed 3.0 am advance billet Coucesion & Rue	
	Routine in billets	
	10th men of ARQUES Ry. Stn. lumbered train S.E. into Channel and placed off rails. Thought despatched & trench mile borough the yard	
17th	morning	
3.34 pm	Regt H arrived orders to hurry ahead at ALLAMONT. Battalion hurrying & marched to MAMETZ	
	Fie. received orders no 193	
19th MAMETZ 2 Am 3rd	Routine in billets	
22nd DATE 160 27th	Instruction transport by train 2nd IC Mann with staff. Brigade moved to N of Railroad of LONGUEVAL	

Army Form C. 2118.

WAR DIARY
or
INTELLIGENCE SUMMARY.
(Erase heading not required.)

Instructions regarding War Diaries and Intelligence Summaries are contained in F.S. Regs., Part II. and the Staff Manual respectively. Title pages will be prepared in manuscript.

Hour, Date, Place	Summary of Events and Information	Remarks and references to Appendices
May 28th 6.30am	Brigade less A. echelon which moved to BRANDHOEK, moved to L'ERKELS BRUGGE arriving 2pm. H.Q. of Brigade. 13 Squadron moved est midroads, B remained attachment to B. echelon remaining at L'ERKELS - BRUGGE. Routine work.	
May 29 - 31. L'ERKELS BRUGGE		

A. Kirkstaple
P.T.O.
Martin W. Bijman

Serial No. 264.

121/6/28

WAR DIARY OF

Transport Officer, Lucknow Cavalry Brigade.

From 1st June 1915. To 30th June 1915.

WAR DIARY
or
INTELLIGENCE SUMMARY.
(Erase heading not required.)

Army Form C. 2118.

Hour, Date, Place	Summary of Events and Information	Remarks and references to Appendices
L'ERKELSBRUGGE June 1st – 12th 1915.	Routine as usual. On 1st 39 Heavy Draught horses which had been replaced by light draught animals, were evacuated. On 3rd 9 light draught animal's with 5 drivers a.s.c were received. On the 5th 6 Heavy Draught horses + 3 drivers were evacuated, which completed the conversion of the Brigade Transport from heavy to light draught animals.	
13th L'ERKELSBRUGGE 14th	Headquarters dismounted portion of Brigade (less A. echelon) billeted Etrick. Brigade marched to MAMETZ area, being joined by A. echelon en arrival in billets. B. echelon marched at 9.20 a.m via ARNEKE – LE MENEGAT – NOORDPEENE – ZUYTPEENE – LESTROS ROIS – STAPLE – WALLON-CAPPEL – LYNDE – BLARINGHEM – ROQUETOIRE to MAMETZ and arriving 5.45 pm.	
MAMETZ 15th – 30th	Routine in billets.	A. Stewart Capt a/c Transport Officer LUCKNOW Cavalry Brigade

fwd.
30.6.1915.

Serial No. 267.

121/6502

WAR DIARY

Transport Officer. Lucknow Cavalry Brigade.

FROM 1st July 1915 TO 31st July 1915

Army Form C. 2118.

WAR DIARY
or
INTELLIGENCE SUMMARY.
(Erase heading not required.)

A.P.'s OFFICE AT THE BASE
No. 1287/W.D.
2 - AUG 1915
INDIAN SECTION

Hour, Date, Place	Summary of Events and Information	Remarks and references to Appendices
MAMETZ July 1st – 31st 1915	Routine duties with the Indian Corps of the month. The Brigade Transport was inspected by G.O.C. 1st Indian Cavalry Brigade, G.O.C. 1st Indian Cavalry Division & G.O.C. Indian Cavalry Corps. Sd/- A.J.Huskisson 31.7.15 Bde Transport Officer Secunderabad Bde.	

SERIAL NO. 267.

Confidential
War Diary
of

Transport Officer, Lucknow Cavalry Brigade.

FROM 1st July 1916 TO 31st July 1916.

WAR DIARY of 8 Bde Tpt. Officer Lucknow Cav. Bde

Army Form C. 2118.
(36)

July 1916

INTELLIGENCE SUMMARY.
(Erase heading not required.)

Hour, Date, Place.	Summary of Events and Information.	Remarks and references to Appendices.
2nd July, 1916.	Reconnoyes "B" Echelon of Bde Transport from GROUCHE to FROHEN LE GRAND	
8th July, 1916	Demonstration of structure of Pontoon Bridge made by 74th Coy. R.E. Pontoons made of 3 G.S. Wagons & Collapsible Boat — carries loads Limbers G.S. Wagons total weight 2 tons.	
10th July, 1916	Limber Hook of Wagon (Limbers G.S.) belonging to 15th Cavalry Dragoon Guards broken. Letter of New Hook pattern No. 35" Good 4 hours to do. G.R.O. No. 15-28 of 19.4.1916. provides certain establishment of spares of these No 35 to be carried by units. Ordnance Dept. issues leaves for holes with no sump are of leaf hooks are not drilled with necessary No. of hinge holes. unless present arrangements of hook stores break on line of march Regt'l Limbers Wagon series have to be left behind to save I time in refitting hook it is suggested that spare hook No 35 "Spares of shackles and 3/8" No. I. Transverse Bag + No. 5/8" Permanently arms in true hook. Hook can readily be fixed up in skeas [?] & mending Orders issued for camouflage act first line transport - hopes I shield painted light brown, conspicuous parts plates and gunwarrel green.	
25th July 1916.		

SERIAL NO. 264.

Confidential
War Diary
of

Transport Officer, Lucknow Cavalry Brigade.

FROM 1st August 1916 TO 31st August 1916.

Army Form C. 2118.

34

● WAR DIARY
or
INTELLIGENCE SUMMARY

Transport Office
Lucknow Cavalry Bde

(Erase heading not required.)

Instructions regarding War Diaries and Intelligence Summaries are contained in F. S. Regs., Part II. and the Staff Manual respectively. Title Pages will be prepared in manuscript.

Place	Date	Hour	Summary of Events and Information	Remarks and references to Appendices
France	6.8.16		Lucknow Cavalry Brigade moves from CHELERS to PAS EN ARTOIS, attached to VII Corps.	
do	22.8.16		Spell of hot weather effects wheels of G.S. Wagons and limbers G.S. Wagons, particularly in regard to wheels. Supplies by Heavy Mobile Workshops, FREVENT, apparently unseasoned timber used in running wheels.	
do	31.8.16		No change	

J Shingel ly Lieut
British Transport Officer
Lucknow Cavalry Brigade
2nd Indian Cav Divn

SERIAL NO. 261

Confidential
War Diary
of

TRANSPORT OFFICER, LUCKNOW CAVALRY BRIGADE.

FROM 1st SEPTEMBER, 1916 TO 30th SEPTEMBER, 1916

Army Form C. 2118.

WAR DIARY
or
INTELLIGENCE SUMMARY B.T.O. Lucknow Bde
(Erase heading not required.)

42

Instructions regarding War Diaries and Intelligence Summaries are contained in F. S. Regs, Part II. and the Staff Manual respectively. Title Pages will be prepared in manuscript.

Place	Date	Hour	Summary of Events and Information	Remarks and references to Appendices
PAS	1.9.16 to 2.9.16		Routine duties	
	3.9.16		Brigade moves to OCOCHES - bivouacs 'B' Echelon at LUCHEUX and marches via BOQUEMAISON	
	4.9.16		Brigade makes again to BRAILLY area, marches 'B' echelon from Rendezvous at BEAUVOIR-RIVIERE	
	5.9.16		Evacuates sick to No 6 Stationary Hospital.	
	6.9.16 to 11.9.16		In Hospital	
	12.9.16		Joined Brigade at HEM -	
	13.9.16		'B' Echelon of Divison marches under O.C. A.S.C. 19 C.D. Rendezvous at BON AIR at 10.30 am. marches via VILLERS - BOCAGE to Camp at QUERIEUX.	
	14.9.16		Left Brigade to take over command of Lucknow G.S. Wagon Train 14 F.K.D.	
	15.9.16 to 28.9.16		O.C. Lucknow G.S. Wagon Train	
	29.9.16		Left HANGEST at 10.30 a.m. in charge of Lucknow Brigade & Divisional stores - proceeds via PONT REMY. advanced troops to AILLY and Bypass to BOIS L'ABBE & area	
	30.9.16		Marches 'B' Echelon [illegible] Bentley Brigade to CRECY.	

[signature]

War Diary.

1st to 28.9.16.

(September) 1916.

Army Form C. 2118.

46.

WAR DIARY
or
INTELLIGENCE SUMMARY
(Erase heading not required.)

Summary of Events and Information

Place	Date	Hour	Summary of Events and Information	Remarks and references to Appendices
SCRAMEN	11/9/16		Hot over 3 limbers F.S. Wagons with 6 mules drew for water. Received rations & supply column 1st M.E.D. so that many carries two days rations for the Persian Levy & Squadron. Rations are on reduced scale and comprise - meat, biscuits, jam, such dried fruit & sugar to Persians atta, Ghee, biscuits such, Jam & sugar for subordinars - no oats for animals. Shortage Types losses are Persian supply system & but Bulham, & but Persian. Our trouble is to keep our cultures for our Persian levy.	
	13/9/16		Introduced scheme into 2 columns & carrying one days rations for personnel - he subsidised each section clothing reverse marches & numbers wagons to each brigade/Squadron route opened Types wagon for equipment storage - only two open supplies wagons in whole team.	
	14/9/16		Males inspection. 3 mules fit to requested supplies clothes etc. One F.S. Wagon sent to "W" Battery to draw stores & medicine.	
QUERIEJ	17/9/16		Moved camp to QUERIEJ - never supply depot V.B.G. B' Echelon. One mile through last. Loss fittings in error.	
	18/9/16		Raining heavily - horses covered as far as possible with Bivouac tarpaulins but much of the rations wet	

WAR DIARY
or
INTELLIGENCE SUMMARY

Army Form C. 2118.

47.

Place	Date	Hour	Summary of Events and Information	Remarks and references to Appendices
DICKIEBUSCH	19/4/16		Received heavily. Sent 1 per mule & Driver to "B" Battery Exchanges return 20 l Rifle (with supply officer for 5 y staff)	
	20/4/16		Ordinary rest day no L Supply officer here by tedium as can be be forwarded. See (Annex)	
	21/4/16		Slice training over. Look had one for 5 by 5 g chg off officer. Slice had to be used before not y trail g true, who did a fine renters draw from "B" Battery 10th.	
	22/4/16		Not war before having hand to Gledow - had only 30 pr available of 2.30 pm to hurd - complete harness & steel Rennie sacks to more with U horse team. When movement order cancelled trained from "B" Batteln orders to be training to remnants.	
	23/4/16			
	24/4/16		German advance in accordance with in Reinforce. So there it have carrier in each limber 200 fruition rounds + 30 a/c each - the other half 20 rounds & 200 driven rations & 1 with life jacket. Carpenter at 9 am have received orders on 5 with divide rifle promotes infants - answer announces game by heard wagon Droce.	

Army Form C. 2118.

48

WAR DIARY
or
INTELLIGENCE SUMMARY
(Erase heading not required.)

Place	Date	Hour	Summary of Events and Information	Remarks and references to Appendices
QUERIEU	26/9/16		Routine duties	
	27/9/16		Orders received for subsequent of Divn. 2nd Echelon to supply Column and rules to obtaining field cases, etc. in exchange for broken grenades. Grenade Coy & permit at 1st Cas. grn. and available. Proceed to 2nd Army Depot Corbie & unloaded. Wagons into Depn. O.C. Depot refuses to take grenades. Unloaded wagons at 11.30. Arrived back in camp at 1.30 a.m.	
	28/9/16		Collects broken grenades & returns into three Wagons - reported same at 1st Divisional Dump. Handed over 59 broken & 58 wagons and teams & escorts together with Grenatier Ordnance Stores, returns in new & unused up to inclusive of 29th Sept. - to Lieutenant Smith, 10th Reserve Park. Reports to O.C. A.T.C 1st Australian Divn. and at PICQUIGNY and resumes duties as Brigade Transport Officer, Indian Cav. Brigade.	

R. Shingfeld, Lieut.
1.10.16

R.L.